MW01231785

Chariots
of
IRE

Barry Parham

ALSO BY BARRY PARHAM

Why I Hate Straws
An offbeat worldview of an offbeat world

Sorry, We Can't Use Funny

Blush
Politics and other unnatural acts

The Middle-Age of Aquarius

Full Frontal Stupidity

You Gonna Finish That Dragon?
Musings from a table for one

Chariots

of

IRE

BARRY PARHAM

Copyright © 2013 Barry Parham
All rights reserved.

ISBN: 14905-56699
ISBN-13: 978-1-490-55669-7

Table of Contents

DEDICATION

This book honors the fond memories of
my grandparents

Janie & Hubert Holbrook
Lila & Bill Parham

---

and this hope:
that our grandchildren
will have an America
as exceptional
as our grandparents' America

Order Now! But Wait!

Didn't they say 'Hurry! Today only!' yesterday, too?
<>~<>~~~~~~~~~~<>~<>~~~~~~~~~~<>~<>

Some people, I've discovered, like to complicate things. Not me. I'm not complicated. I'm just a simple guy, with simple dreams and simple desires: some food, some books, a ridiculously large music collection, and some more food. Just keep it simple, and don't confuse me.

Commercials confuse me. Though, to be fair, lots of things confuse me. Al Roker's appeal, for one thing. People who get excited about lawn care, for another. How vampires went from scary to sexy. Neckties. Okra.

Why is black-and-white Tarzan's hair slicked back, and with what? Who did Adam and Eve's sons marry? And why #2 pencils? What happened to all the #1 pencils? Did somebody use them all up stabbing vampires? It's confusing.

I remember when commercials were easy. Some polite human with sand-blasted teeth would point to a product, strongly suggest you buy it, and then shut up. Nice. Simple. And no drippy gore on any undead teeth.

But commercials these days are obtuse and obscure, like some conceptual foreign film. A nasal duck with a limited vocabulary attacks a kid delivering Chinese food: buy our insurance! An anthropomorphic frog mourns on its lily pad, surrounded by an amphibian 'misery management' support group: buy our beer! Sometimes you have to watch a commercial several times (and you'll get to) before you figure out what they're selling.

And then there are the commercials that don't even attempt to sell you *anything*. They're just on a PR binge: they just want you to *like* them. You know the type:

Here at Global Offshore Sweatshops, we don't make the skateboard: we make the skateboard faster. We don't make the bat: we make the bat harder, so we can sell the bat to thug kids in street gangs who've outgrown skateboards. We don't make the computers: we make the casings that coat the nails that fasten the shelves that line the walls that house the computers that are hacked by the thug kids who then steal your identity and, on weekends, hit people with bats. Here at Global Offshore Sweatshops, we don't make the stuff you buy: we make the stuff you buy hurt you.

So let's look at some examples. I'll describe actual ads that companies have produced and aired on TV, and you tell me what product these people are wanting you to buy.

...if you can...

Ready? Good luck!

~~-~~-~~-~~

A driver with an expensive non-American car and chiseled facial features is barreling down the middle of a middle-of-nowhere straightaway. Suddenly, a military support plane screams into view, extends its mid-air refueling snake, and refills the driver's coffee cup.

Order now! But...*what?*

a) A new car
b) An after-market sunroof
c) An ego reduction kit

A bubbly woman in white works in a stark white, horizon-less store that houses stark white shelves packed with vague, colorful boxes. Her name is Flo, she's a part-time biker, she has a merry-go-round, and she's often visited by guardedly nervous men who wear light blue suits and have no spine.

Order now! But...*what?*

a) Car insurance
b) Wimp repellent
c) Dr. Seuss's new book, *'Horton Hears an Emasculated Who!'*

A young Asian-looking woman sees air bubbles in a store aquarium. A young Indian-looking man sees workers mixing up concrete in a wheelbarrow. A young soccer mom sees kids having a water balloon fight. They all rush home, fire up an online conference, and prototype a brilliant water delivery system that looks suspiciously like a cement-spackled party favor in a fish tank.

Order now! But...*what?*

a) Online conference software
b) A super-sized pallet of paper towels
c) A Toys-R-Us 'My First Aqueduct' kit

A cocky, evil man who goes by the unlikely name of 'Mayhem' and is indestructible (you just don't get cockier than *that*) gets hit by a train, bounces off your car, gets electrocuted, is sucked through a large, bladed farm implement, gets attacked by escaped mental patients wielding #1 pencils, and ends up crashing through your roof.

Order now! But...*what?*

a)   Property insurance
b)   An ethics-optional, results-oriented realtor
c)   A machine-washable anti-Mayhem parka

A lady wants to quit smoking. We know how badly she wants to quit because she takes long walks with her boyfriend and her kids do their homework in the kitchen. A disembodied announcer's voice recommends she try a product that has absolutely nothing to do with smoking. On the plus side, however, the product can cause "occasional, discomforting side-effects" ranging from dry mouth to suicide, including medical conditions so vile that we won't discuss them here, but they rhyme with 'spectral breeding.' In rare cases, totally innocent dogs in entirely different neighborhoods may spontaneously explode.

Order now! But...*what?*

a)   Anti-depression medicine
b)   Pet-store-issue *"Now - in your time of loss"* sympathy card value packs
c)   Another parka

A grizzled man's aging muscle car overheats in the desert. Oddly enough, this happens near the only gas station within 450 miles. At the station, the man grabs a bottle of water, refills his radiator, and drives away. He never bothers to speak to the equally grizzled proprietor. We're pretty sure he didn't pay for the water, either.

Order now! But...*what?*

a)   Sexual dysfunction medicine
b)   Three online global activists who prototype water delivery systems
c)   Eight weeks of etiquette classes

A father and daughter are shooting hoops in their driveway, accompanied by a giant imaginary tiger that's standing on its hind legs and grinning like Al Roker on assignment in Phoenix. They finish and go inside for breakfast. As they eat, the tiger stands in the background, grinning and yelling about something being great. Other than a red bandanna, the tiger is stark naked.

Order now! But...*what?*

a)   Breakfast cereal
b)   Tickets to the annual 'Fauna in the Sauna' safari at the Playboy Mansion
c)   Anti-psychotic medication

The walls in your home are being attacked by a computer-generated monster that looks like something Stephen King might have dreamed up one night after eating too much pizza.

Order now! But...*what?*

a) Pest control
b) Martha Stewart's new book, *'101 Affordable Ways To Entertain In A Condemned Building'*
c) Stephen King's new book, *'Stomach'*

A wealthy lady takes a decorative plate from her curio cabinet, grabs a hammer, and smashes the plate, causing her maid to momentarily stop cleaning. So the lady fires the maid, then logs in to Monster.com and reactivates her ad: 'WANTED: Unappreciated menial to do condescending work for insulting wages. Preference given to illegals who hail from predominately Catholic countries.' The lady then grabs a shard from the shattered china, runs to the museum, and uses it to repair a painting.

Order now! But...*what?*
a) Investment funds
b) A robot floor sweeper
c) A robot floor sweeper with a Catholic accent

There's a battle for Earth. A pudgy, mute animated character is slinging tires at a giant marauding gas tank. The giant gas tank has monstrous tentacles, each terminating in a gas nozzle. It's hard to pinpoint the mute animated character: he could be the puffy white mascot from a tire company in France, or that giant grinning nautical marshmallow man from 'Ghostbusters,' or a mid-winter Barney Frank.

Order now! But...*what?*
a) Document-management services
b) Barack Obama's new book, *'How I Liberated France'*

c) A flex-fuel vehicle with the 'Marauding Giant Collision Alert, and Floor Mats' option package

A man in an unbelievably cheap suit and what is, hands-down, the world's worst hairpiece, looks directly into the camera and asks you several times if you've been injured.

Order now! But...*what?*
a) Legal services
b) A handgun and several rounds of ammunition
c) O.J. Simpson's new book, *'I Didn't Injure You, But If I Had, Here's How I Would Have Done It'*

~~-~~-~~-~~

Well, I hope this little exercise helped better prepare you for America's unending, ongoing onslaught of TV commercials. After all, in the Battle for the Wallet Bulge, you need to gird your loins, although that could chafe your ... um ... girdage.

And when you get to the *' enough TV already!'* stage, give me a shout. I can get you a sweet deal on a bat.

Louisville, that is...not vampire.

How To Run a Planet

America faces new challenges...and that's just our leadership

<>~<>~~~~~~~~~~<>~<>~~~~~~~~~~~<>~<>

Sometime during the summer of 2012, some guy in California released a movie clip on You-Tube.

And immediately, all over the planet, nothing happened.

True, this little-known film clip had promising potential to be a trouble-maker. The clip contained 'religious' references that might offend people in countries where they have sand sidewalks. Also, the director of the movie had spent the bulk of his cinematic career churning out smutty gems like "The Sexpert" and "Young Lady Chatterley" (I *and* II).

But the point is, nothing happened. For months, nobody, anywhere, cared. Life went on. In America, people rationed their TV time between watching football teams out-injury each other, watching presidential candidates out-insult each other, and watching a 6-year-old kid named Honey Boo Boo smoke fake cigarettes and drink real Red Bull.

And then, in September, an anti-America anger volcano erupted in practically every country where people wear open-toed shoes and eat chickpeas.

So, naturally, the White House issued a statement, lamenting the riots that had somehow manifested in over a dozen countries at the same time, and blaming the sudden violence on that film clip from last summer.

And then the President flew to Las Vegas to attend a re-election fundraiser.

Then we got word that rioters in Tripoli had destroyed a Hardee's, a move that threatened to set the Libyan economy back by several years. (An adjoining Kentucky Fried Chicken franchise was also attacked, but the rioters were foiled after the KFC's clever night manager deployed a canola oil slick.)

So, naturally, the White House issued a statement, lamenting the deaths of thousands of defenseless Thickburgers, and blaming the fast food massacre on Paul Ryan's budget.

And then the President flew to New York to attend a re-election fundraiser.

Now, to be fair, it's not easy being President of the USA, *and* Commander-in-Chief, *and* Leader of the Free World, *and* to still maintain a golf handicap of 18. Plus, when you finally *do* get a few minutes at home alone, there's all those armed men walking around on your roof.

Think you could do better?

Well, let's find out. We've put together a little quiz, to see how President You would stack up against the guy that's there now.

Let's see how *you* would handle the pressure of juggling all things Presidential: things like effecting hope; deflecting blame; projecting your chin while simultaneously biting your lip and displaying your profile; pinching your thumb and forefinger together and making little up-and-down pointy gestures; trying to keep a straight face while giving an acceptance speech in front of a bunch of fake Greek columns.

Ready? Let's begin.

~-~-~-~-~-~-~-~-~-~-~-~

What do you call an eruption of self-destructive mob violence in an Arab nation?
- A predictable reaction to decades of desperation
- A culturally-fed alternative translation of religious texts
- Thursday

~-~-~-~-~-~

Within 72 hours of the first incident, US embassies from Africa to Indonesia were under attack. As America's Fundraiser-in-Chief, what do you blame it on?
- A 3-month-old movie clip
- Mitt Romney noticing that US embassies from Africa to Indonesia were under attack
- Maybe not everybody has seen your Nobel Peace Prize yet

~-~-~-~-~-~

Because you're too busy campaigning for re-election, you blow off all those pesky Daily Intelligence Briefings; instead, you just watch a short PowerPoint presentation and skim through a how-to primer (*Religious Fascism for Dummies*). Finally, you agree to return the Pentagon's phone call, and the Joint Chiefs present you with a full slate of Chief Executive options. Which option will you select?

- Direct military intervention
- Crippling economic sanctions
- A five iron

~-~-~-~-~-~

A Cairo protestor is caught on camera, showing his displeasure with America in the usual way - by stomping up and down on a sign written in German. What will be the most likely reaction from world governments?

- France surrenders to the sign
- Qatar purchases Cairo
- Greece asks Qatar for a loan, offering to write a post-dated check
- Qatar purchases Honey Boo Boo

~-~-~-~-~-~

When attempting to convince voters of your global qualifications to lead America, what will be the centerpiece in your display of competency?

- Your years of familiarity with the geopolitical disciplines

- Your decades of depth in the intricacies of international law
- Your Al Green impersonation

~-~-~-~-~-~

Regardless of his crisis - or his historically consistent failure to manage them - the President can always blame somebody else. Any target in this list will do, but which is your favorite?

- The Bush recession
- The Bush tax cuts
- The Bush stock market
- The Bush job market
- The burning bush
- Bush's Baked Beans
- Bush Hog rotary cutters (single- or multi-spindle)
- Kate Bush
- Republicans
- Earthquakes
- Republican earthquakes

~-~-~-~-~-~

Congress, meanwhile, rather than face any difficult decision-making in an election year, actually voted for an *increase* in spending. What tactic might make them wake up to some fiscal realities?

- The imposition of term limits
- An intensive, long-term series of town hall meetings
- Having their knees removed

~-~-~-~-~-~

During this heated political season, which of these phrases might now be taken as a racist slur?

- Health care
- Chicago
- Niggardly
- A salad bar with freshly-sliced cantaloupe
- It's a trick question. These days, every word in the English language can be taken as a racist slur.

~-~-~-~-~-~~-~-~-~-~-~

See? Being President's tougher than you thought, huh? So don't be too quick to blame this one.

After all, he's only superhuman.

Death by Ennui

If an armed bad guy attacks, just hit him with your free
phone

<>~<>~~~~~~~~~~<>~<>~~~~~~~~~~~<>~<>

It all started when Maury yelled, "Go long!"

Rob set down his cup and sprinted across the postage stamp of a lawn. Maury zeroed in and fired an absolute bullet. Rob bared his teeth, juked to the left, and went airborne, his arms straining to capacity in an effort to pull in the rifled spira...

"Hold it!"

And that's when Dianne Feinstein showed up.

The dour, distaff Senator wormed her way out of her limo, this one comped for her by lobbyists from MADAMS (Mothers Against Dangerous Analogies, Metaphors & Similes). She thudded across the driveway, enclosed in a cotillion of lawyers, a pack of aides, and one doctor from the IRS. (Bureau of Sports Injuries, Touch Football Division, Sundays, Smallish Lawns)

Maury stared at the entourage, completely at a loss. *Feinstein?* He mused. *California Feinstein? How'd she get in this humor column?*

All he could imagine was that he'd stepped out of the pocket, maybe crossed the line of scrimmage. Maybe somebody'd ratted him out for nursing an oversized soda. *But I'm in my own yard!*

"Young man," dripped the Senatrix, as her bobbed hair didn't wave in the breeze. "Don't you realize that you can no longer say words like 'bullet' or 'rifle' in public, now that my Anti-Bad Stuff legislation has made violence illegal?

"It wasn't me! That was the guy who *wrote* me!"

He had a point.

"That wasn't *violence*," Maury reasoned. "That was just, I don't know, exposition. Set-up. Heck, it wasn't even *dialogue!*"

Feinstein raised her eyebrows. Her slitted eyes never left Maury's as she slowly cranked her chin skyward, from Doubtful, past Confrontational, all the way up to Self-Righteous.

"*Rifle. Bullet.* See the pattern?" lectured the Senatress. "I know, I know - just seemingly harmless football analogies, right? Sure, that's where it starts. But words like *bullet, rifle, offense* - those are gateway words. Soon, it's not enough. You want more; you want stronger words; words like *'conflict'* or *'Huck Finn'* or even *'To Kill a Mockingbird.'* Before long, you're reading unapproved novels by Kurt Vonnegut and Tom Robbins. And next thing you know, you're on a downtown rooftop, wearing camo and face paint, and yelling Tom Clancy quotes at innocent civilians."

"That's not your business, you meddlesome twidge," Maury shot back. (Figuratively, he shot back. Not literally *shot back*, of course. Maury's in enough trouble already.) "Who do you think you are?"

Feinstein bristled, except for her hair. "I am a United States Senator," she proclaimed, in large bold type. "I've had my portrait painted and everything."

"Doesn't matter," countered Maury. "I have the right to say 'shot back,' or to bear arms, or to say 'bear arms,' or to buy an iPhone even though I know full well there's a new model coming out next month. Those are my inalienable rights!"

"But you're not an inalien. You were born here."

For a moment, Maury could only blink. "You're kidding, right? Did you maybe hit your head getting out of the limo?"

"Don't change the subject."

Rob trotted up and nudged Maury. "Yo, Maur. Who's the hair helmet with the Brooks Brothers posse?"

Feinstein pursed her lips and tried to look indignant, which was nearly impossible in that pantsuit. A barely perceptible nod of her head, and a swarm of black-spectacled agents had Rob on his stomach, frisking him for concealed Quentin Tarantino videos, or novels by Zane Grey. The IRS doctor checked Rob's pulse, consulted a chart, and ordered a battery of invasive, non-covered renal exams, and a knee replacement.

The agent with his own knee on Rob's neck flipped Rob's smart phone to Feinstein. She looked at the music app and clicked her teeth. "I see you've downloaded some music by Guns N' Roses."

"Hey, I got a permit for that."

Feinstein turned to an aide. "Take a note: introduce legislation to force that band to change their name to something less threatening. *Blunt Scissors N' Roses*, maybe."

"Excellent idea," toadied the toady.

"Scare up a Republican to co-sponsor the bill. Preferably from the South. See who's up for re-election, dangle the quid pro blah blah blah - you know the drill."

The aide saluted. "Yes, sir or ma'am."

One of the agents stepped up to confront Maury. "Sir, your associate has in his possession a potentially moral-altering MP3. In keeping with the provisions of the Feinstein Anti-Bad Stuff law, we're gonna have to refurbish the Senate's bowling alley, and raise your taxes."

"Wha...raise *my* taxes? What are y...but *Rob's* the one with the music that might eventually cause him to commit a random act of senseless violence!"

"Sir, your friend is temporarily exempt from Federal prosecution, due to his pending knee replacement."

"Mmph nn mmk krmmph," Rob added.

He had a point.

The Senatorette oiled back to her limo, then paused and turned. "Remember," she recited, "if we can save just one vote. Just one."

Maury helped Rob to his feet, helped him hose off the IRS residue, and then looked around at his familiar neighborhood.

No. *Formerly* familiar.

Across the street, Fred Johnson was animatedly instructing his family on how to use an unfolded paper clip to fend off an armed home invader. Tacked to Ted Baker's porch next door was a sign Maury hadn't noticed before: a universally-recognizable red circle with a line drawn through its middle, riding above these stenciled words: THIS IS A METAPHOR-FREE ZONE.

Inside the circle was a book.

The bullet-proofed MADAMS limo lurched away from the curve, its armor-plating barely avoiding a giant splotch of irony. "Welcome to the new normal," curdled the more-or-less female voice behind the tinted window.

Maury could think of only one thing left to try. He walked to the end of his street, and then walked some more. He walked until he came to the tacked lip of thin canvas. Maury peeled back the veneer and stared intently into the middle distance until he spotted what he was after: the title and credits of this story. *There he is*, Maury exhaled. *That's the guy.*

"Barry! Hey, *Barry!* Get me out of this!"

So I did.

The End

Post-Teenage Wasteland

Later. I'll grow old gracefully later.
<>~<>~~~~~~~~~~<>~<>~~~~~~~~~~<>~<>

Some of you will remember The Who. I guess. I hope. Thanks to The Who, my generation learned many of life's invaluable coping skills, like guitar smashing, amp puncturing, and how to be deaf.

But, for those of us who grew up in the late 20th Century, their contributions went way beyond simply broadening our corporate skillsets.

The Who was one of the defining rock 'n' roll bands of my generation; in fact, they penned one of the teenage anthems of my generation, entitled ... well ... *My Generation.*

Remember?

People try to put us down (talkin' bout my generation)
Just because we get around (talkin' bout my generation)
Things they do look awful cold (talkin' bout my generation)
I hope I die before I get old, else the medically ignorant bureaucrats at the
IRS might decide I'm not allowed to replace my out-of-network spleen
based on some arcane spleen reimbursement cost analysis that isn't covered

because some half-stoned civil service twidge in the ObamaCare Auxiliary Organ Management Department (Spleen Subcommittee, Out-Of-Network Branch) misspelled the word 'bile' (talkin' bout my generation)

My Generation was recorded in 1965. And *that*, children, was a long time ago, in case you've misplaced your smart phone and can't get to the math app. Way back then, America only had three TV stations, two genders, and one allergy (Communism).

Now it's 2012. Fully half The Who have gone to that great record store in the sky; down here, Roger Daltrey is 68, Pete Townshend is 67, and I'm now at the age where, instead of staying up till dawn, I try to stay awake till dark.

And this past week confronted me with a couple of things that brought on a bout of nostalgia:
1. America survived another Presidential election, which I went through with the rest of you - in fact, according to some vote-counters in Florida and Ohio, more than 100% of you.
2. Here in the South Carolina upstate, The Who performed live; however, this year, the audience's drugs of choice were Ben-Gay and No-Doz.

But for those of you who when I said "The Who" said "the *who?*" - I've ~~set you up for~~
I've set up for you a quick Late Twentieth Century trivia quiz. Ready?

~-~-~-~-~-~

Who was Ella Fitzgerald?

a) A jazz singer without equal
b) An overzealous Cape Cod coed who married President Kennedy's middle name
c) The guy who wrote *'The Great Gatsby'*

Who was Captain Kangaroo?
a) The first President of Australia
b) A famous soldier who was killed during a duel with Colonel Mustard
c) The common-law wife of Captain Crunch

Who was Johnny Carson?
a) The patron saint of Malibu
b) The common-law wife of Ed McMahon
c) Wasn't he, like, that Indian scout dude and stuff?

Who was Monica Lewinsky?
a) The founder of Who's Your Papa John's Pizza
b) A character in Ella Fitzgerald's first novel, 'The So-So Gatsby'
c) The creator of Maryland's first combination dry cleaning & discount birth control drive-thru
d) The inspiration for the submissive female lead in the very popular risqué novel, 'Fifty Shades of Depending On What You Mean by the Word Grey'

Before the internet and email were invented by Al Gore, how did people share jokes?
a) People used to get all their jokes from watching what were called 'variety shows' - what we know today as 'network television news.'

b) Before the internet and email, it wasn't possible to share jokes, because nobody knew how to say "LOL."

c) What do you mean, 'before the internet?'

Next to the '0' on the number pads of late-20th-Century telephones were the letters OPER. What did OPER mean?

a) OPER was short for 'Operative' - during the Nixon administration, pressing that key connected you with the CIA agent who was monitoring your phone calls.

b) OPER was an acronym created by the phone company. They never told us what it meant, but federal laws mandated that it had to be there on everybody's phone, much like that mysterious 'do not remove this tag' warning on your mattresses.

c) OPER was short for 'Opera.' See, in the late 20th Century, the economy was fantastic, so every household had their own phone, indoor plumbing, and a live-in Italian chorus.

Why does the South Carolina "Education" lottery have the insipidly lame marketing slogan, "Have you scratched today?"

a) This is not really part of the quiz. I just had to get that off my chest.

Before music was invented by Al Gore, what did people do at concerts?

a) Not a whole lot, really. Not until Al Gore invented lighters.

b) Bands would just cut straight to the guitar smashing part.

c) People just stood around counting to four, over and over again, wherever Al Gore had created festival seating. 1, 2, 3, 4, 1, 2, 3, 4, over and over in a subdued, anticipatory kind of way. And then came ... the waltz.

Whose music best defines the late 20th Century?

a)   The Beatles, before they broke up

b)   The Beatles, after they broke up

c)   Cat Stevens, back when he was still a heathen

d)   Madonna, before she broke down

What was the name of the first ever portable music device?

a)   The eight-track tape

b)   A radio, if you stole it

c)   The iPod iPhonograph (*optional i45 iSpindle not included*)

d)   Dick Clark

How did the eight-track tape system work?

a)   We're not sure, but it was way better than the seven-track tape system.

b)   Tiny little musicians rode around in a molded plastic rectangle. Actually, in the 60s, stuff like that happened more often than you might think.

c)   You shoved this plastic container into a hole below your car radio, and music came out. Then you rode around for a while singing along, until it stopped working. When it stopped working, you folded up a matchbook and shoved it in under the eight-track tape. That made it work again. No, really.

d)   I'm dead serious.

What was the best thing about eight-track tapes?

a)   They nearly always often worked sometimes.

b)   They single-handedly revived the struggling matchbook industry.

c) It was really cool when the plastic case melted all over your car's dashboard.

d) Eight-tracks were so lousy that when cassette tapes came out, we thought they were magic from Mount Olympus.

What's the worst thing about digital music in general?

a) Trying to figure out where to stick the matchbook

b) I get tired of writing checks for 99 cents.

c) You can't play them backwards and pretend like you hear secret messages.

d) Ever tried to roll a joint on an MP3?

~-~-~-~-~-~

Well, I hope that little challenge gives you young people a deeper appreciation ~~for your superiors~~

~~for your betters~~

~~for your elders~~

for those of us who, despite being just a wee bit older, are still wise, amazingly clever, and startlingly attractive.

Not to mention humble to a fault. Go in peace.

One last note for the record, cause I don't want anyone to get any wrong impressions, especially anyone who's still on the phone from the circa-Nixon CIA: that little joke I made about rolling a joint on an MP3?

Just a joke. I gave up experimenting with MP3s years ago.

Survey Says?

You know, they say 42.8% of all statistics are made up on the spot.
<>~<>~~~~~~~~~~<>~<>~~~~~~~~~~<>~<>

This year, while watching politicians racing around trying to out-slime each other, I've been struck by their ability to turn statistics into schizophrenics. It's scary, but it's fun to watch - a politician can make a four swear it's a five, or a three, or a five again, and do it while simultaneously kissing babies, straddling fences, and going all Artful Dodger on your wallet.

Now before you get antsy, know that this is *not* a piece about politics. Well, at least not directly. Every year, it seems, politics creeps a little bit closer to the rest of us, over here out of the spotlight, futilely yelling, "No! We're just fine, thanks. Go make a bridge or something. Invade somebody, whatever. Really, we're just fine. But thanks for asking!"

Someone famous once said, "All politics is local." Of course, someone else once said, "Hey, babe, be a dear and play *'Helter Skelter'* again while I carve a swastika on my forehead," and *he* was famous, too. But let's not get sidetracked on J. Edgar Hoover's senior prom.

As you probably know, that "All politics is local" quote is attributed to the famous statesman and former live person, Tip O'Neill, who regrettably passed away before telling anybody what the heck it meant. Grettably, though, the quote seems quite close in spirit to "All sewage is local," a phrase coined by my sister's cousin's half-brother, the highly respected Tony One-Lip. Tony is our local Commissioner of Cement Projects, Garbage Pickup, and In-Law Vetting, as well as the owner of *Sinistro Amico*, a 'rapid response' service agency. ("Car-Trunk Steam Cleaning, While You Wait!")

Politics: if you got the pearls, we got the swine.

But that's not for today. No, today, we're here to talk about issues of import. Things that may affect us on a multi-generational level. The great topics of the ages. To wit:

- Statistics as a bellwether of our society
- The importance of unbiased baselines in non-manipulative probability and its potential interplay with the Central Limit Theorem
- Whole milk

Like me, you might be surprised, initially, at the sheer volume of statistics available online about a topic as pedestrian as milk. But remember where we are - and *when* we are: we live in 21st century America, where "OMG LOL" is a complete sentence, and people have *American Idol's* phone number on speed dial. And if *that's* not an argument for steadily increasing levels of mandated medication, I don't know much.

So let's dive into milk. (sorry) In 2005, Americans drank 2.7 billion gallons of milk. (The latest data we could find was for 2005; apparently, that's the last time Al Gore updated the internet.) By the way, one gallon of milk weighs 8.6 pounds, in case you're planning to bring a few gallons on the plane as carry-on luggage, and with my luck, you'll have the seat next to me.

Young boys tend to drink milk 10% more often than girls, which is why it's called a "milk moustache" instead of, say, a "milk lip-gloss spritz." And 9.1% of you out there drink an entire gallon of milk every single day. (Not only will you be seated next to me on the plane; you'll be in the window seat.)

FUN FACTOID: One milk-based site offered a handy list of links to other on-topic websites. One of the milk-related topics? Corrective lenses. Apparently, chugging a whole gallon of milk a day can not only make you go *often*, it can make you go *blind*. Which puts a whole new spin on "lactose-intolerant."

Just next door to milk on the food chain is cheese. In 1909, Americans nibbled just north of 3 pounds of cheese per person, per year. By 2001, we were up to 30 pounds of cheese a year. At this rate, by 2050, we'll all be George Wendt. Homeland Security is looking into the problem, and Congress has summoned several of the usual suspects to appear and testify, including Domino's Pizza, that Sargento guy, and Little Miss Muffet.

FUN FACTOID: This massive bloat (sorry) in cheese consumption also led directly to me creating several dairy-product-related jokes, none of which I'm proud of.

Nationally, we're no better with butter, either. In 2004 (the last year anybody's cholesterol was low enough to allow for running around, counting stuff), we collectively spread 1,353,000,000,000 pounds of the stuff on stuff. That statistic alone ought to make you proud to be an American, or two. But count those zeroes - that's 1.35 *billion* pounds of butter, scooped and dolloped onto biscuits, gravy, corn, and, for all I know, other butter. After all, to reach that rate of consumption, we could've been slathering lard on carport walls, pets, and Tip O'Neill.

People are just getting larger and larger; in fact, according to a recent survey, 2 out of 3 people are now 3 out of 4 people.

They've even come up with a new word to describe American over-eating, and all its attendant medical problems: Diabesity.

Ladies and gentlemen, welcome to Diabesity! Because sometimes, gluttony just isn't enough.

There is a side-order (sorry) of good news, a bit of bright-ish lining. We're eating more fish, according to statistics. But you can't really trust some of these reports. A footnote points out that the numbers exclude "edible fishery products consumed in Puerto Rico," but include tuna caught by foreign vessels in American Samoa.

Yes. You heard me correctly. That's what we're getting for our tax dollars - we're paying all-growed-up adults to count tuna fish sandwiches. Undocumented Samoan tuna fish sandwiches.

But now let's walk past the food (sorry) and study some other statistics, like crime. In 2009, according to US Census numbers, 1,000 males were arrested for the nebulous-sounding crime of 'suspicion.' (No females were arrested for suspicion in 2009. I don't know why, but I'm willing to bet lip gloss was involved.)

So a thousand guys were run in for suspicion. But on the same report, in the 'Totals' category for the same offense, the number somehow swells (sorry) to 1,600. That can only mean one thing: those guys not only got fatter- they got fatter *while the report was being written.* Maybe they were arrested for suspicion of switching to whole milk.

FUN FACTOID: According to crime statistics, if you're an Alaskan native, you are 45 times less likely to be a runaway then the rest of us. Maybe it's too cold. Maybe there's something about moose meat that they're not telling us down here.

If you live in the South, statistics say you're 14% more likely to smoke pot, but if you live in the West, you're 36% more likely to get popped for cocaine. In fact, in California, your chances of getting arrested for possession of an "other dangerous narcotic drug" are four times higher (sorry) than the rest of us. This condition is what is known in behavioral science classes as a "critical social meltdown," and to residents of Malibu as a "buffet."

And speaking of drugs, the number of arrests for methamphetamine between the years 2000 and 2009 has dropped by 35%. However, the *amount* of meth seized in those less-frequent arrests has *gone up* by 75%. And if that's not a testament to workplace efficiencies in the American capitalist model, I don't know much.

And then there are the statistics that are simply confounding. Interestingly, and I use that term with a straight face, Americans *import* less timber than before, but we also *export* less timber. And I don't think I have to tell you what *that* means: the analysis is indisputable. As a country, we're simply eating less wood.

Be prepared, though, as you surf statistics, for some disappointments. For example, the most current timber industry numbers for Western hemlock stumpage prices (as expressed in constant dollars) are not available. Douglas fir stumpage prices have gone missing, too. Downright sloppy, is what it is. As taxpayers, we have a right to expect more. Perhaps our Justice Department will look into it, as soon as they get out of prison.

FUN FACTOID: To be honest, I really didn't lose a lot of sleep brooding over those missing hemlock numbers. But if you think I'm gonna miss an opportunity to say "stumpage prices," you don't know much.

Auto Suggestions

Car: a $30,000 box used for storing two bucks in loose change

<>~<>~~~~~~~~~~<>~<>~~~~~~~~~~<>~<>

I've never been the type that gets excited about cars. I realize that confession could jeopardize my standing as A Guy, but there it is. In my opinion, automobiles have a very short *'What Good Are You?'* list. For me, a car is:

- A device for getting to food, or for getting food brought to me
- A way to irritate rabid environmentalists
- A 'fast food packaging' museum with wheels

Once upon a time, it's true, cars came in handy when you needed to go buy something you *weren't* planning to eat, like furniture, or cauliflower. But ever since Al Gore invented the electron, we don't have to actually go to stores to buy stuff, we can enjoy vacations virtually, and for communication we can chat, text, Skype, IM, email, poke and tweet. (Heaven forbid we should have an actual face-to-face conversation with a person. We might have to make eye contact!)

So cars don't do much for me, personally, although I do understand the huge role that cars play in our economy: we buy cars, so car dealers can buy boats, so boat dealers can buy cars. It's like the circle of life, but with less raw meat.

On the downside, however, cars have lots of drawbacks:

- Cars are insanely expensive, but don't let that put you off. After you own it, only the *parts* are insanely expensive.
- The parts have mysterious names like the differential, the alternator, the terminator, the heir filter, the wallet extractor, the static impotent bombastic emissions desculptifier, and the limited warranty.
- The parts break.
- The parts that break are usually expensive. If they're not expensive, they're not in stock. If they are in stock, there's another minor catch. (see 'limited warranty')

And the cost of cars, the ceaseless spending, hits you everywhere. Parking, for example, which is an absolute racket. Recently, a traveling friend asked me to pick up her car at the airport and keep it at my place. No problem! So a friend from work drove me to the airport, less than two hours after her flight flew, to pick up her car.

Less than two hours, mind you.

Nice Parking Lady: Ten dollars, please.
Me: Shut up.
Eternally Smiling Parking Lady: Ten dollars, please.
Me: Did the car commit a crime or something?

I ponied up, paid off the pleasant extortionist, and moved along, trying to remember why I'd ever wanted a driver's license in the first place.

The first car I ever owned was a second-hand Buick Electra 225 - the legendary *Deuce and a Quarter* - the safest civilian vehicle ever invented. Driving in a Deuce was as close as any youngster would ever get to being bulletproof. That car weighed more than my current house.

And then, one day, as I was driving along a neighborhood street and trying to kiss the defenseless girl in the passenger seat, the car drove into a ditch for absolutely no reason whatsoever.

Looking back, though, there might have been other fates at work. Cosmic forces. Kismet. On another moonlit evening, as I attempted again to kiss the same girl as we sat in *her* car, a large tree branch fell through her rear windshield. (That was around 1972. Oddly, she hasn't returned any of my calls since.)

And despite all the annual screaming about "this year's model," cars haven't really changed much since then. Shorter, lighter, a few more toys. Generally speaking, cars are quite standardized, so that any idiot with a pulse can drive one in several lanes at once while eating fast food and sending text messages and not noticing that his turn signal's been blinking since the Korean War.

I don't want to get overly technical here, but at its core, a car has a door, a seat, and a place on the steering column to insert a key. (Although I was once stymied by a Saab. I nearly starved to death before I spotted the sadistic center-console keyhole. But the day wasn't a total loss - I did learn how to curse in Swedish.)

Beyond the seat and the key, and maybe the radio, it's probably best if you don't think too much about how a car works. Probably best not to dwell on the details, like the fact that you're barreling down the freeway in a device that has more than 10,000 moving parts, powered by what are, in essence, liquefied dinosaur parts that participate in over one hundred explosions every second, all enclosed in an aluminum box built by bitter Union workers who smoke pot at lunch and can't be fired.

But for a piece of metal that explodes for a living, cars evince odd emotions in people. For example, a person you've never met will actually walk up to your car and finger-spell "WASH ME!" on one of the windows. Only cars can get humans that fired up about filth. Nobody ever paws "POWER-WASH ME!" on your house, or wipes "WASH ME LOL" on your workstation monitor. People don't run around crop-circling "MOW ME!" on unkempt exurban lawns.

Speaking of filth - ever been to the car wash and had to make that toughest of all decisions? You know the one: when you pull your car in and the Car Wash Option Lady - that leathery, raspy matron with the peroxide updo, the bangles and the dangling cigarette - when she asks you what après-wash 'scent' you want?

And it's always the same three olfactory options: Pine Forest, Pina Colada, or New Car. Why don't they offer more realistic (or better yet, more adventurous) aromas?

- Toxic Melted Dashboard Ornament
- Morgue Elevator
- Recirculated Hirsute Wrestler B.O.
- Incontinent Elder Relative
- East German Olympic Locker Room
- Potentially Fatal Gas-line Leak
- Windowless Downtown Cigar Bar
- Mid-August Post-Soccer Carpool
- Yes, I Believe She Did Use The Entire Bottle Of Perfume
- Stale Child

Who are they kidding? Who, do you suppose, is ever fooled by New Car Smell? Picture it: you pull up at your date's house in your 1984 Dodge Dart, a car that's spewing more foul smoke than a Middle-Earth Balrog. You haven't changed the oil in this road whale since Captain Kangaroo was issued his first odd little conductor's jacket. There's duct tape on the upholstery and masking tape crisscrossed on the ceiling. A sun visor pendulums as you open the car door with a pair of adjustable pliers. And then, as you shoehorn your date, Totie, through the plastic-patched hole that once was the passenger-side window, she inhales a cloying nostril-full of New Car Smell and fawningly sighs, "Ooh! New car?"

Okay. Maybe Totie's fooled. If so, take it as a sign. Call the caterer, scribble up the pre-nups, and I hope you two will be very happy together.

Hmm. And you thought *cars* were expensive...

Southern Exposure

Crisis management: check. Now we just need a crisis.
<>~<>~~~~~~~~~<>~<>~~~~~~~~~<>~<>

Winter. Here in South Carolina, like in most places, winter happens every year, usually during the winter.

Not to get technical, but I think winter happens this way: a weak stationary occluding geothermal front collides with shifting low-level temperate cumulo-isobars, or a sullen rain god, resulting in the formation of complex adjectives. This produces a 95% chance of citizens getting storm-crowed into a meteorological panic by incredibly tanned weatherpeople named Angelique d'Portofino, or Chad.

Duly warned, we Southerners then brace ourselves for...

...up to almost nearly a quarter-inch of snow.

And then, as regularly as clockwork, we go insane. Power outages. Bread and milk shortages. Pitifully unprepared pine trees snapping like Hillary at an ethics investigation. A run on batteries and generators, a vertigo-inducing spike in rear-end collisions, and the obligatory local news segment on how to turn your Ford F-150 Hemi Dually Rally SVT EcoBoost

Raptor into a makeshift snow plow with just a toss of vinyl siding and some duct tape.

But we know when we're in for dangerous days, because the forecast will get upgraded from "snow" to "a snow event." So says Chad Packet, the Chief Weatherologicalist over at Extra-Massive Insta-Chart Mega-Uber-Doppler Live-Forecast-4-U Weather, and Chad should know, because he has a parka, and tanned hair.

Now, Northerners always scoff at our Southern winters, because Northerners regularly attract snowfall at depths that have to be measured with taped-together yardsticks...and that's just the *August* snow.

But that's the point, isn't it? As you yourselves say, you get 27 dozen feet of snow every year. So you, and your cars, your trees, your electricity; you're all used to it.

And then there's this: you Northerners *know* you're gonna get 27 dozen feet of snow, every year - but you still refuse to leave. You keep living there, year after year, until you reach the age when, by law, you have to move to Florida, wear plaid shorts and black knee socks, and learn how to order bagels in Spanish.

So don't lecture *us* on intelligence. You and your uppity indoor plumbing.

But for those of us down here, stuck in this annual arctic nightmare, we've put together a few helpful tips for surviving The Southern Blizzard.

How To Prepare For A Blizzard

- At the first hint of winter weather, your responsibility is to ensure that your family has enough white bread, milk, and Burt Reynolds' movies to get you through the society-interrupting effects of the blizzard, which could very easily last till mid-morning tomorrow.

- Keep in mind that this is a thermal emergency. This is no time to get cute with the groceries. This is a life-or-death situation, and it wants whole milk. Don't be bringing home skim milk. Don't walk in with milk that's 2% fat or low-fat or no-fat; organic, neo-organic, or BST-free; alleged milk allegedly made from nuts, rice, soy, or spelt; or any of those bogus milk-like milk substitutes targeting the colonic needs of the lactose-intolerant, that are painstakingly prepared in a stress-free recycled-adobe ashram by pale, peasant dress-dressed oxo-vegan wiccans named Tori and Khaitlynnh.

- (I'm trying not to make a joke about "crying over spelt milk." I really am. But it's hard.)

- Don't forget, however, to supplement your survival menu with something beyond just milk and white bread, especially if you ever want your children to speak to you in public. Chips are good; cookies are better. If you forget, no worries. Just outside the grocery, there's a 105% chance that you'll be gang-marketed by diminutive Girl Scout Cookie pushers, strategically positioned between you and your car.

- Oh, and here's some advice: if you ever decide to buy from the Girl Scout Cookie barricade, and the Girl Scout Leader lady is obviously attracted to you, it's probably not a good idea to agree to meet her for a nightcap at the Gray Wolf Karaoke Bar and Full-Contact Cocktail Lounge.

• Don't ask.

How To Drive In A Blizzard

• Driving in bad weather is like any other perceived threat to the male ego. The key is confidence; aka, "yelling." You have to remind Mother Nature who's boss. Take charge. Yes, we know: you can't actually *yell* at Mother Nature - your fallback position is obstinate bull-headed stupidity. Real men don't cautiously test roads or timidly tap brakes. And checking weather forecasts, like asking for directions, is the type of activity meant for those little fruit cup-eatin' fellas who say "I'll just have the salad bar" - *even when the menu has hot wings* - not guys who hunt wild boar with a bow. (no arrows, mind you - just a bow)

• When the roads are covered with snow or ice, the preferred way to drive is to barrel down the road as fast as possible. It all boils down to math, really: the faster you drive, the less time you're stuck out there in all that bad weather without any white bread, or beer.

• Alternatively, you can choose to savor the sub-arctic experience and just inch along at eight miles an hour. Remember, it may not snow again in your lifetime, so enjoy the scenery! Plus, all the drivers stacked up behind you will be really impressed with your calm serenity. (In fact, they'll be so overcome with admiration, you'll probably see them gesturing wildly as they break out in impromptu forms of interpretive dance.)

• In traffic, be sure to pull up as close as possible to the truck or car in front of you. That way you can take advantage of the heat emitted from that vehicle's exhaust pipe(s). And if the lead car goes fast enough, you can draft. If you don't know what "drafting" is, you're not really *from* the South, are you?

• Keep in mind that, in a blizzard, colors can be deceiving. White-outs aren't, and black ice isn't. Red light means skid; green light means spin; yellow light means what it's always meant in the South: a dare. "*Hey!* Yeah, *you!* Any second now, the traffic on both side streets is gonna be squealing out into your lane, like a wild boar on Automatic Weapons Day. Any second now. So go 'head. *I dare you.*"

• Before leaving for work, be sure to check the local TV news for school and business closings. If you have no electricity, understand that repeatedly slapping the side of your TV will not make it come on. If you're not sure your electricity's out, flick on the light switch and run straight across the room at full speed. If you hit something, either your power's out or you're very stupid. If you're that stupid, you shouldn't be bothering with a job - you should be running for Congress.

• No, it is *not* a good idea to pour bourbon in your radiator. Yes, I understand that your grandfather referred to whiskey as "antifreeze," but your grandfather also once called the cable company because he couldn't find the Coco Chanel. Remember: your grandfather's idea of fine dining is fish sticks, he thinks Archie Bunker was too liberal, and due to that tricky episode with the Girl Scout cookies, he's still not allowed back in the state of Virginia.

Don't ask.

Love Me (Chicken) Tender

Why you should wait an hour after eating before you read the news

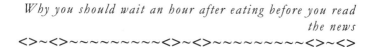

This week, while you and I went about our normal routines of apologizing for working hard and being successful, the world was busily attending to its own mission: to be even more silly than last week.

And, as usual, the world found a way - as documented by a bevy of bizarre, media mania-fed events, like accusations of dead pets voting, the story of a Nigerian guy who got gang-wifed, and the transgendered breakfast wrap boycott at Taco Bell.

I made that up, of course. Nobody's boycotting anybody's breakfast just because of the sexual orientation of a tortilla. That would just be silly.

Wouldn't it.

But America was prepared to go even sillier than that. So let's set the week's mood:

This week in London, the 2012 Olympic Games began with Team Australia getting lost on its way from the airport, which was not all that surprising, given that NBC News confused Australia with Austria. Next, there was an uncomfortable national flag mix-up between those madcap neighbors, North Korea and South Korea, the Hatfields & McCoys of the Pacific Rim. And America's athletes were seen parading around in some bizarre, one-world fashion combo of Catholic school uniforms, Continental Airlines flight attendant scarves, and French berets, all made in China.

In exurban Denver, a guy put on a costume and shot seventy people, was arrested, showed up in court with orange spray-painted hair, ignored his lawyer, sat in the jury box, and then dozed off. So local authorities are watching him closely for signs of...ahem...abnormal behavior. Apparently, it takes quite a bit to be considered abnormal in Colorado. Maybe it's the altitude. After all, where I live, some people think I've a loose screw just because I believe the universe was created.

Elsewhere, a non-profit group in Virginia was being questioned for sending out voter registration teasers to dead people and pets, actor Steven Seagal was being sued over the death of a pet dog, and US President Barack Obama said he ate a dog.

That's how bizarre this week has been. You *do* realize, don't you - I'm several paragraphs in to this, and I haven't had to make anything up yet.

Okay, I *did* make up the part about the Continental Airlines scarves. Scarves are no longer allowed on planes that weigh more than 12 ounces.

But the absolute cherry on this week's Cake of Kooky has been the fried chicken firestorm about Chick-fil-A: a sprawling story of hate, intolerance, and heterosexual chicken biscuits.

Here's the back story, in a nutshell: in an interview with Dan Cathy, the calm, sane CEO of the wildly-successful Chick-fil-A food chain, Cathy expressed his personal opinion in favor of traditional marriage. Then he shut up and went home.

And so, of course, since the gentleman had hurt absolutely no one by stating his personal opinion, he and his entire enterprise were immediately pilloried by protesting crowds of non-traditional-marriage advocates, armed with posters, magic markers, and terry-cloth chicken suits.

And now, all that "Be tolerant or I'll hate you" tolerance threatens to derail one man's entrepreneurial dream, a simple, timeless dream shared by so many of us: the opportunity to sell a piece of chicken and, with any luck, tick off Rahm Emanuel.

And so, here, presented in no particular disorder, is a list of news stories. Some of them aren't entirely true. But that's your only clue.

~-~-~-~-~-~-~-~-~-~-~-~

The Mayor of Boston has accused Chick-fil-A of serving heterosexual fried chicken, non-union waffle fries, and cage-raised buns. (According to an unsubstantiated rumor, the buns may also be hot, or cross, or both.)

~-~-~-~-~-~-~

To protest a restaurant executive having a personal opinion, some activists are planning to hold what they're calling a same-sex kiss-in.

In a repulsive counter-offensive, supporters of the restaurant have collectively threatened to buy a chicken biscuit.

~-~-~-~-~-~-~

Chicago's Mayor Rahm Emanuel says Chick-fil-A's values are not "Chicago values," and is trying to block the restaurant's commerce options in the Windy City. Chick-fil-A cleared the City Hall hurdles, though, after they arranged to have six pullets murdered, tossed a Treasury Department's biscuit in Lake Michigan, and pimped out two bags of waffle fries.

~-~-~-~-~-~-~

According to a press release, action actor Steven Seagal has purchased a new facial expression. Seagal, who is also a producer, guitarist, a reserve deputy sheriff, and an incredibly bad standup comic, reportedly bought the expression from Al Gore, who had several expressions still in their original packaging. The purchase now gives Seagal a range of three expressions: stoic anger, pensive hesitation, and that feeling you get when you bite into a bad oyster.

~-~-~-~-~-~-~

The Chick-fil-A controversy continued to heat up today, and is now spilling over into other franchises. Al Sharpton has accused Colonel Sanders of being an antebellum racist, citing an encrypted lyric allegedly uncovered while listening to several bluegrass albums played backwards. Sharpton also pointed out that the Colonel wears white suits. (And we would like to point out that if the Reverend ever has a sanity hearing, he should try to have it in Colorado, if you catch our drift.)

Upon hearing that the franchise's spokesman is a Colonel, Ron Paul demanded that we get all our troops out of Kentucky.

~-~-~-~-~-~-~

New York City's Mayor Bloomberg has shared his two cents on the Chick-fil-A phobia-fest, stating that it would be unfair to penalize a business simply because its CEO supports primitive mating rituals, like traditional marriage, or fidelity.

However, continued Bloomberg, guests who wish to make a toast at traditional wedding receptions in New York must use wineglasses no larger than 12 ounces, and the city will no longer allow brides to be "biggie sized."

~-~-~-~-~-~-~

In response to the anti-chicken protests, a conservative group, the One-Rooster-One-Hen Coalition, has demanded that cable TV providers immediately discontinue all Hanna-Barbera cartoons. The demands came after the offended activists learned that Fred Flintstone was allegedly having a gay old time.

~-~-~-~-~-~-~

Due to the poor economy, gas prices, record drought, and rises in associated costs, restaurants whose recipes use meat saw their stock prices plummet. Taco Bell stock soared.

~-~-~-~-~-~-~

Today in Arizona, a Chick-fil-A was picketed by a group of transgendered illegal alien cows wearing misspelled sandwich boards. When things got out of hand, Sheriff Joe Arpaio wheeled in and arrested six Catholic nuggets.

~_~_~_~_~_~

A splinter group calling themselves the Liberal Activists for Moronic Ennui (LAME) has sued the chicken wings giant, Hooters, demanding that the popular bar & grill only offer left wings.

~_~_~_~_~_~

Yesterday, Roseanne Barr may have expressed her opinion on the Chick-fil-A story. Or maybe she didn't. Nobody cares about Roseanne Barr.

~_~_~_~_~_~

In an anti-marriage editorial, Alternative Lifestyle advocates pointed to a "cautionary tale" from Africa, in which a Nigerian man was allegedly forced to have sex with all six of his wives, a dubious household chore which allegedly killed the man. Friends enviously recalled a consistently chipper fellow who, in-between constantly conjugating verbs (among other things), was regularly required to not mow the lawn or fix the sink, forced to lie on the sofa all day and eat slice after slice of delivery pizza while not wearing any pants, and made to watch hour after hour of televised football.

In related news, politicos were quick to point that Mitt Romney's grandfather had had twelve wives. This may or may not have any bearing on candidate Romney's qualifications for public office, but I think we can all agree that it makes Grandpa a masochist.

~-~-~-~-~-~

Supporters of Chick-fil-A suffered a major setback today when animation legend Foghorn Leghorn was outed by Yogi Bear, who admitted to being 'on the rebound' after a messy breakup with someone known only as Mr. Ranger Sir. The pronouncement came during an impromptu pic-a-nic lunch with Yogi, who wore a tasteful porkpie hat but no pants. The imaginary rooster's bold statement was considered a victory, not only for chicken pride, but for domesticated and feral partners in trans-species relationships everywhere.

~-~-~-~-~-~-~-~-~-~-~

So there it is. That's the kind of week we've had here in America, where all menus are created equal, and every citizen has an inalienable right to lifestyle, puberty and the pursuit of moderately-sized soft drinks.

And in case you were wondering what our government's been up to during all this controversy, here's a final food-related story:

~-~-~-~-~-~

A recent edition of the USDA's employee newsletter is promoting, among other things, something they call "Meatless Monday." Apparently, though, USDA management have a seriously low level of confidence in the cognitive skills of their employees, because in the sentence just after the Meatless Monday announcement, the USDA felt the need to clarify that the effort "encourages people not eat meat on Mondays."

So what we have here are civil servants that can't grasp a complex phrase like "Meatless Monday." Maybe they can attend a taxpayer-funded seminar in Vegas or something. Imagine *that* class:

Instructor: "In other words, on the day after Sunday, you should eat things that aren't cow-shaped."

Tenured USDA Drone: "Is this gonna be on the test?"

Suspension of Belief

Life imitates art. Art retains counsel, sues life. Film at eleven.

<>~<>~~~~~~~~~~<>~<>~~~~~~~~~~<>~<>

Sometimes it's awfully hard to write satire. Why? Because I'm not fast enough.

It's crazy. And it's scary. I'll dream up something so ridiculously ironic, so deliciously stupid that there is *NO WAY* it could ever actually happen. No way anybody would do it.

And then, before I can grab a pencil and paper, I hear on the news that somebody did it.

Here, I'll show you what I mean. Pretend for a minute that I was ever clever enough (I'm not) to conjure up any of the following absurd scenarios:

- A celebrity attorney will agree to represent the girlfriend of a guy who ate another guy's head.
- Team sports will begin to bore the detainees at the Guantanamo Bay Maximum Soccer Field Facility For Terrorists Who Forgot To Light The Fuse In Their Underwear. So American taxpayers will be asked to pony

up so the detainees can attend classes on *How to Write a More Effective Résumé.*

- China will launch its own space station, and release a political prisoner who, apparently, is a blues singer.
- A government spokesman will argue that a teenager working part-time at a record store qualifies as a "green job." The spokesman will say this while under oath, *and* with a straight face, and nobody will tackle him, clap on restraints, and ship *him* off to Gitmo.
- Two words: Cat seatbelts.

Now suppose I came to you two weeks ago with *even one* of those ideas as the basis for a humor column. You'd nod politely at me, excuse yourself for a moment, then grab the phone and call one of those shrubberied, gated facilities with a name like Somnolent Green and a discreet fleet of steel-reinforced vans, with the cup holders and seatbelts replaced by handcuffs and jaw restraints. (It's a special after-market option package: the passive-aggressive restraint system. Additional options include a full-moon roof, Thorazine mini-bar, and a set of floor mats that must be seen to be believed.)

But this is not fiction - *this is the news.* This stuff is actually happening. Take, for instance, the "green job" story.

In reports and at hearings, deeply-flawed federal flunkies are thrumming their harps and claiming that the Obama administration has created something like 467 contraskillion "green" jobs. Apparently, they've not only managed to gainfully employ every mammal in our galaxy, they've also managed to put all those mammals to work watering windmills and harvesting solar-powered soy burgers. And having done so, they've now pushed on out, creating jobs in previously uncharted universes, which might explain where they got their hyper-math calculator.

But when asked for the proof behind the numbers, they begrudgingly admit to playing a bit loose with the statistics. For instance, when counting their way up to "green," it turns out they were counting:

- Janitors who worked at Solyndra
- People who eat salads
- Employees of book stores that carry Dr. Suess's *Green Eggs & Ham*
- Mr. Greenjeans, Graham Greene, Kermit the Frog, and the Incredible Hulk
- The staff at amazon.com, and their entire customer base, since they still stock VHS copies of *Green Acres*
- People who are supporters of Greenpeace, or supporters of whales, or supporters of athletics, or supporters of athletic supporters
- Anyone who's ever read *Mill on the Floss*, or visited a mill, or reminded their children to floss
- People who have envy issues
- Six beauticians who visited a Georgia theme park and had a bad experience involving a roller coaster and some undercooked pork
- Cartoonists who draw the Green Lantern comic strip (they're awarded *double* liberal points for that one, now that the Green Lantern's gay)
- Ireland

And then there's the news from China (or as they're now known, Bank of America). While our own government was busy running for re-election, running from responsibility, and running around emasculating NASA, the Chinese arced their own space station into Earth orbit, to see if their Manhattan real estate purchases were affected by zero gravity. Crew members from the International Space Station immediately called over to say 'hi,' and to order some carry-out.

Reliable sources say the Oriental orbiter will be named either Panda Garden, Great Wall Garden, Happy Panda Garden Wall, or Tibet North. And the folks at Guinness claim it's the only man-made all-you-can-eat buffet in outer space that can be seen from Earth.

Currently, the station is unmanned, but China has plans to send up some astronauts very soon, who will do a good job or else their relatives will be executed. This was corroborated by the Chinese dissident and blues singer, Cheng Melon Chitlin. Cheng was just granted political asylum in the United States, which qualifies him to run for President, and in-state tuition. Cheng, now a resident of New Jersey, is best known for his soulful rendition of the Percy Sledge classic, "Tiananmen Loves A Woman."

Speaking of the Garden State - if you're driving in New Jersey and your pet isn't wearing a seatbelt, you could face a $1000 fine. But if *you* or some other insignificant human is caught not wearing a seatbelt, the fine's less than fifty bucks. So your best bet is to buckle up, kick back, and let the dog drive.

(By the way, it occurs to me that 'if you're driving in New Jersey' may be the most redundant remark ever made.)

Just make sure Lassie has all her papers (sorry), license and registration, and no priors. You don't want any legal trouble. All the non-indicted lawyers are busy suing the Governor of Wisconsin for getting elected. Twice.

And of course the celebrity attorney in the story ... in *every* story ... is that ubiquitous, permeating pain in the nexus, Gloria Allred. Of course it is. That woman's chased so many ambulances, her nose has tail-light burns. She's the only human in history to have her teeth registered as a trailer hitch.

Mizriz Allred, who was recently inducted into the Real Yellow Pages Refrigerator Magnet Hall of Fame, has a gift for starring in unusual stories. She's like Johnny Depp, but with less eye makeup. Her latest crusade appears to be a nosy, dilettantish diatribe to remind everybody that cannibalism is bad, a claim that was immediately refuted by Fred Txltetloptltxan, chief counsel for the Dade County Mayan Anti-Defamation League.

Had you heard? Cannibalism is bad.

According to several news reports, the valiant Litigatrix hustled up a news conference and made the following observation: "Cannibalism is a serious issue and is very dangerous to the health and the well-being of the cannibal and the victim."

Cannibalism is dangerous to the health of the victim.

Go ahead. Admit it. Hadn't thought that through, had you? The legal lady's pronouncement is one of those tired, obvious, I-Did-Not-Need-To-Be-Told-That klaxons, like "Do not use this vacuum cleaner while sleeping" or "Friends don't let cats drive drunk."

On the other hand, let's not be too hasty. Think Green. Between cannibalism and all the Chinese going to outer space, we could solve overcrowding in no time. And now that pets are driving, they can jolly well go pick up their *own* Alpo and Kal Kan, so we're no longer needed there. A bit of controlled cannibalism might just save the planet.

Besides, it's the *absolute* last word in recycling.

Crime Spree in the Carolinas

A man. A gun. A pig on the run. It's the stuff of legends.

<>~<>~~~~~~~~~~<>~<>~~~~~~~~~~<>~<>

For me, as an observer of America, it was one of those perfect moments.

"...after the pig had been pardoned..."

Whoa.

If you've ever tried to write a weekly humor column, you know the feeling of exhilaration that accompanies the discovery of really odd news. That rush that rides in on the wave of something unbelievably senseless. These are moments you live for.

And this was one such moment.

According to a local news report, a citizen of South Carolina has been charged with assassinating a fugitive celebrity pig.

I suppose I could just stop right there. To paraphrase the brilliant comic, Lewis Black, at this point I could easily just pause for a beat, say "Thank you and good night!" and walk off the stage. End of show.

But then you'd never find out about Maggie and Peaches.

This globally repercussive story broke in the coastal South Carolina township of Meggett, which, as every schoolchild knows, was once the home of the Palmetto State's second-largest fish cannery. (*Make your travel plans now!*)

Now, the town of Meggett is situated deep within what South Carolinians call the "Lowcountry," the mossy-oaked, waterway-laced coastal part of the state where I was born, long ago, back before mankind had many of its modern, common conveniences, like opposable thumbs.

I'm not exactly sure how Meggett is pronounced, because in the South Carolina Lowcountry, pronunciations can get pretty weird. Over several centuries, unique dialects have evolved...dialects like Geechee, Gullah, and Andy Griffith. This *lingua franca* is a rich paste made of exotic ingredients: African, European, Caribbean, American, even French Huguenots (literal translation: *large rude astronauts*). And the end result was weirdness: 'Simons' pronounced *Simmons*; 'Manigault' pronounced *Manna-Go*; 'plough' pronounced *pluff*; 'surrender' pronounced the way it's usually pronounced in France.

But now, crime has come to the mecca that is Meggett. In these dark days, it seems, not even this intercontinental idyll is immune.

According to a deputy's incident report, a 26-year-old Meggett local shot and killed an 800-pound escaping pig, after spotting the fugitive somewhere along Ethel Post Office Road. (Ethel herself avoided getting caught in the crossfire, despite being a woman apparently large enough to warrant her own post office).

The decedent, a brown and pink ex-pig named Maggie, was being housed at LEARN, a non-profit organization dedicated to caring for abused farm animals, and other victims of Congressional misbehavior. Maggie allegedly went over the wall along with another trouble-maker, a recidivistic side of bacon going by the name Peaches. (possibly an alias)

Initial reports claimed Maggie was the former mascot of a local grocery chain that, for years, has somehow managed to call itself The Piggly Wiggly while keeping a straight face. Later, however, an official spokeswiggly clarified Maggie's role as that of poster pig for "National Pig Day," a pig pardoning promo emphasizing the vital role South Carolina plays in the production of pork, and funny chain store names.

And then, after getting pardoned, Maggie was sent to the aforementioned Old Farm Animals' Home, located just up the road a piece from the aforementioned megalopolis of Meggett.

You can find Meggett on a map, but you will *have to*. Meggett, South Carolina, is not one of those places that just suddenly loom and blot daylight, like Atlanta, or Marlon Brando. Arriving in Meggett won't happen by accident. It's not like when you're barreling along the freeway, distracted in deep conversation with your passenger, and then suddenly there are shadows everywhere, you start mumbling "Atlanta? How'd we get *here?*" and you forced to focus on navigating an eighteen-lane freeway gauntlet, dodging discarded furniture pallets, meteor-sized slabs of 18-wheeler tire tread, and embittered Braves fans.

Oh, no. You have to *want* to go to Meggett.

Not that you *shouldn't* want to, of course. Meggett is a "thriving" community (*source: Ethel*) with a "bounteous" history (*source: Ethel's thesaurus, I'm guessing*) and a "vibrant" downtown featuring several "paved" roads. The downtown Zone of Vibrancy even features a large merchants building, in case any large merchants stop by.

Founded in 1905 as an eventually historic coastal railroad town, Meggett was the first municipality in America created solely for the purpose of eventually becoming historic. Meggett is home to 1,226 Meggettitians, according to the 2010 US Census, though that figure has dropped over the last decade from 1,230. (Four people, possibly lost during the Great Grit Famine of 2001.)

That same Census calculates that "minorities" make up about 17% of Meggett's population; looking deeper into those numbers, we see that the 17% includes a few "Asians," even less "Indians," somebody known as an "Other," and 0.9% that are mysteriously referred to as "Two."

The citizens of Meggett, including Ethel, Other, and Two, are served by a Town Council form of government. The Council meets monthly, in the produce association building, except during months when anybody invites any large merchants. Each month, residents who wish to be placed on the agenda must submit their request in writing, though waivers are available for the literacy-challenged, like four-footed felons, and public school students.

And as if being erstwhile home to South Carolina's second-largest fish cannery weren't reason enough to crow, Meggett was at one time hailed as Cabbage Capital of the world. Thanks to its historical coastal railroad, Meggett cabbage was shipped out to points far and wide, from which points most of it was shipped right back.

Yes, shipped back. Don't act surprised. Remember - it may be Cabbage Capital of the World cabbage, *but it's still cabbage.*

Eventually, the railroad depot started donating all that tonnage of rejected cabbage to the LEARN geriatric pig farm, which may help explain why disgruntled grunters like Peaches and Maggie finally decided to make a break for it.

And that turned out to be Maggie's last mistake.

The deputy's report noted that the 26-year-old Meggett male saw Maggie running in and out of the road near Ethel's, a pattern of behavior which, the deputy had to agree, would be considered unusual for an 800-pound pig *or* Ethel. The alleged male then allegedly went home, grabbed a gun, and immediately raced in to town to register as a Republican.

The shooter later told deputies that he'd been motivated by concern that Maggie would cause an accident; however, witnesses at the scene of the assassination say they overheard the gunman making plans to drop off all 800 brown and pink pounds of Maggie at Manigault Meats, a local slaughterhouse and micro-brewery.

According to the news report, no official charges have been filed against the shooter; however, the pig's owner was warned that, at the time the incident took place, Maggie was considered "at large" and in violation of county ordinances.

At this time, the whereabouts of Peaches, Maggie's former partner in crime and current ham on the lam, remain unknown. Law enforcement officials have issued an All Porks Bulletin, a Hamber Alert, and a very wide-angle mug shot.

And finally, though we cannot confirm this, sources close to the sow say that Peaches has reached out for simpatico legal counsel. If and when the time comes, the pig will be represented by celebrity attorney Gloria Allred.

State Bored of Education

Is this, like, gonna be on the test and stuff?
<>~<>~~~~~~~~~~<>~<>~~~~~~~~~~<>~<>

Okay. Just before I started running for the exit, here's what the gothic-eyed little mall rat said to her equally doom-daubed friend: "I'm, like, so totally un-into it and stuff."

And then, suddenly, without warning, her orbiting mascara cloud hit critical mass and achieved self-consciousness. The mascara-based life form immediately pulled out a smart phone and started texting.

Unfortunately, due to my being busy running away, I never did find out exactly *what* had failed to stimulate the child's imagination...what it was the naïf waif was so un-into. Maybe English was, like, her second language and stuff.

I had only just made it out the auto-doors when the mall's Muzak system started blaring that Gangnam-style song, the one some sadistic deejay has apparently decreed must be played every eleven minutes. I peeked back inside the mall and, right on Pavlovian cue, the food court was filled with arm-flapping, duck-walking, hormone-gnashing young adults, with multiple body piercings and single-digit IQs, who simultaneously broke out in a Gangnam-style psychotic episode, while texting.

So what happened to our education system? When did we take this nose dive? In a recent list of the Top 50 Smartest Countries, we're, like, sixtieth and stuff.

It's hard to get a consensus on the *problem*, much less a solution. Teacher Unions think the answer is to ensure that teachers can keep their jobs forever, regardless of petty benchmarks like being competent, or having a pulse. Student advocates advocate for smaller class sizes, despite the lack of any empirical proof that smaller students are any smarter than the large ones.

And we *definitely* can't look to bureaucrats for answers - when it comes to problem misdiagnosis and solution mangling, government is still the undisputed World Champion. As we speak, California is considering dropping arithmetic from the time-honored "Three Rs." (Maybe the third R will be replaced with "*Riding around, texting.*")

In some New York State schoolrooms, students are no longer disciplined for bad behavior - for things like cursing out, like, the teacher and stuff.

So these educators are ignoring actual, real bad behavior; meanwhile, schools elsewhere are cracking down on imaginary depravity. In Colorado, a seven-year-old second-grader has been suspended - *suspended* - for pretending to throw a grenade.

For pretending to throw a grenade.

"Take virtually *that*, you not-really-there bad guy!"

Fortunately, the fake grenade didn't not go off.

But the fledgling scoundrel wasn't done yet...oh, no. He also - now hang on to something - he also made a "boom" sound.

Yes. It's true. During recess, a child made a sound effect.

I say we have him publicly caned.

To be fair, I suppose we can't blindly blame the schools for overreacting. I guess they have to do *something*; after all, some college kids are getting dangerously close to graduating and moving back in with their parents.

So let's peer into the beast. Here at the Weekly Mooncalf, our researchers have uncovered an actual second-grade test, lest you think kids are, like, learning nothing and stuff. These are sample questions for seven-year-olds, from an exam that's actually being administered in classrooms across the country, as far as you know.

Ready? Let's begin.

~-~-~-~-~-~-~

Please choose the most appropriate word to complete the following analogy: Fish is to ocean as chicken is to...
1.   barnyard
2.   very shallow wading pool

3. The French Revolution
4. Colonel Sanders

Sam says that 1/3 of a pie is less than 1/4 of a pie. Is Sam correct?

1. Sam is incorrect, but telling him that might scar his sensitivity, or damage his inner adult thingie.
2. Sam's not supposed to eat pie. Sam has blood sugar issues.
3. Today, Sam says 1/3 is less. But at last week's news conference, Sam was on record as saying 1/3 is more. That's why Sam is class president. Again.
4. Sam is incorrect. We'd hold him back from second grade, but Sam is already 47 years old.

What was the main topic during the famous Lincoln-Douglas debates in 1858?

1. A bowl game between the Ole Miss Rebels and Union Carbide
2. The 1858 *American Idol* finalists
3. The French Revolution
4. Whether or not new territories would have unlimited texting

At school on Monday morning, Johnny has three apples and fifty cents. Billy has two apples and seventy-five cents. Sally has no apples. On Tuesday morning, Sally has a dollar and change, and five apples. What timeless economic principle is at work here?

1. "supply and demand"
2. "distribution of wealth"
3. "neo-classical post-Keynesian analytics"
4. "work that skirt"

The three branches of America's government are
1. Executive, Legislative, and Judicial
2. Executive, Hourly, and Custodial
3. Congress, Progress, and Digress
4. Broken

The mass of a clothespin is 9.2 grams. What is the total mass of 1000 clothespins?
1. The total mass is an Our Father and three Hail Mary's
2. What the heck is a clothespin?
3. The French Revolution
4. Grams? Cumulative mass? Stop it! I'm only seven!

A Congressman's male assistant is most often referred to as
1. An aide
2. A page
3. An unindicted co-conspirator
4. Lucy

Pick the number that is 1000 more than 56821.
1. 56822
2. 56821000
3. The cumulative mass of Colonel Sanders
4. 1000 more what?

According to some scientists, the movement of vast land masses is caused by
1. Plate tectonics
2. Global warming
3. Refried beans
4. George Bush

Purnell painted 1/4 of his home room's door gray. How much of the door remains unpainted?

1. The other 1/4.
2. All of it. Purnell was using imaginary paint.
3. About 3/4. Which'll still be waiting for Purnell when he gets out of reform school.
4. Seriously, his name is Purnell?

A sign says "NOW SERVING VALUED CUSTOMER 379." Can you figure out what this means?

1. It means you're at the Department of Motor Vehicles, it's 4:50 pm, and you're holding Valued Customer Reservation Voucher #28,414.
2. It means you've somehow traveled back in time, and you landed at the grand opening of the very first McDonald's.
3. It mean you're customer 380, and customer 379 will undoubtedly stutter around like she's never before in all her 67 years been involved in a financial transaction that involved writing a personal check and presenting some form of identification, which is buried somewhere in the bowels of her Buick-sized purse. Oh, yeah - and she forgot - she has these coupons, too.
4. It doesn't mean much. That sign hasn't worked in my lifetime.

Sally has $1.25 and five apples. Then Sally bought another apple for $0.52. How much money does Sally have left?

1. Sally has 73 cents left, which means Sally's net worth is 71 cents larger than California's state government.
2. Sally still has $1.25, because she borrowed the 52 cents from Purnell.

3. Sally now has several million dollars, which she received in federal farm subsidies after discovering a tax loophole and having herself classified as a struggling apple orchard.

4. *Another* apple, she bought? Are we talking about Sally or Snow White's evil queen?

On Saturday, it started snowing at 12:30. Where would the minute hand be at 12:30?

1. C'mon, Teach. Really? I'm seven, but I'm not *stupid*.

2. Great. That figures. On Saturday, it snows.

3. The *what?* Did you say the *minute hand?* Let me guess - your Mom still uses clothespins.

4. Leave me alone, already - it's Saturday!

A number is missing from the pattern 25, 50, 75, 100, ___, 150, 175. Can you solve the mystery?

1. Ooh. What a poser. Thought up these questions all by yourself, did you, Euclid?

2. I don't know, but if the missing number looks anything like an apple, I'd haul in that fruit freak, Sally.

3. Why are we trusting you with our children? You can't even keep track of six or seven numbers.

4. I'm guessing Sam stole it.

~-~-~-~-~-~

Tricky, huh? So maybe this whole education dilemma has more horns than we realize.

Personally, I'm more worried about the infamous Colorado Grenadier, that ordnance-lobbing little seven-year-old. I just hope he learns his lesson and gets back on the Straight and

Narrow before it's too late. Otherwise, we know how it all might end. We've seen it happen too many times.

Imagine this kid, ten years later...

"I'm in for Grand Theft Auto and Aggravated Assault. What'd you do?"
"I said 'boom'."

Hard Time Loves A Hero

Sports idols belong in a line-up. But not this kind of line-up.

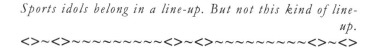

"Well, they say time loves a hero, but only time will tell.
If he's real, he's a legend from heaven; if he ain't, he's a mouthpiece from hell."
Little Feat

~-~-~-~-~-~

If you follow sports news, this last week should've kept you pretty busy. If you follow *weird* sports news, this last week should've charged you a fee...a fee you should've gladly paid. And left a nice tip.

Ready for the latest from the Weird Sports News department? Try this on:

A 22-year-old named Ronaiah Tuiasosopo convinced a football player named Manti Te'o that he, Ronaiah, was a woman named Kennay Kekua, who had a sister named U'ilani. The football player fell in love with the imaginary woman, who later faked dying to death from imaginary leukemia, causing Notre Dame to lose to Alabama.

Here's the weird part - I didn't have to make any of that up...even such highly suspect monikers as Tuiasosopo, U'ilani, and Alabama.

And speaking of unindicted people with aliases: explain *that* to me. Tuiasosopo? U'ilani? Why do these types of stories never involve people named Sally, or Tom? Somebody should look into this.

(International observers were quick to point out that the previous paragraphs are guilty of about eighteen different violations of the UN's "Silly Name" Conventions.)

Of course, besides Manti Te'o mourning over his non-girl girlfriend who didn't really not die before Notre Dame did not win, there's other sporting news. We're still trapped by the seemingly inescapable saga of Lance Armstrong and his parade of adjustable confessions. "Did not! Did so! Did, too!"

And those are just *his* versions of the story.

It's as if the man had two heads - which, given the tonnage of biped-altering dope he allegedly did and didn't take, is a distinct possibility.

Then, this last week, Lance showed up on one of the forty-seven Oprah niche channels to announce that he's never actually told the truth about *anything* since, oh, the year he learned to write in cursive. But today he was going to tell the truth. No, really.

(gigantic thrumming noise)

(that disturbance in the force was the sound of millions of channel changers being power-clicked, as droves of disenchanted viewers switched to the Oprah Weather channel)

Here's a new flash, kids: there is dishonesty in professional sports.

Huh? When did *that* start?

Look: Professional sports, after all, are just collections of humans, and therefore are corruptible, and therefore are corrupt. Pro sports have been corrupt since history's first recorded playoff, when the Philistine Jawbones hosted the visiting Canaanites, and Goliath - everyone's pick for that year's MVP - was sucker-punched by a ringer, an underage rookie named David.

So greased sports is not exactly a recent phenomenon. In fact, America's very first baseball team was involved in a game-fixing scandal. Remember?

The first-ever baseball team in America, the Cincinnati Red Stockings, took to the field in 1869. But sadly, nobody had invented any other teams yet. (The stadium owners were furious, since they were stuck with all those peanuts and crackerjacks.) Shortly thereafter, the team changed their name to the Cincinnati Reds and the players sold their stockings to some nearby politicians, resulting in the creation of Ohio's first female impersonators.

Then came the 1919 World Series, where professional crime met professional sports in the infamous "Black Sox Scandal," an illegal game-fixing scheme involving shady characters and criminals from...hang on to something...Chicago.

The Black Sox Scandal involved the Chicago White Sox throwing their Series against the Cincinnati Reds, who still wore red stockings despite the name change, and despite there being a team in Boston named the Red Sox, and by now you can't help but notice Major League Baseball's unhealthy fixation with footwear. Somebody should look into this.

Eventually, all the Chicago players involved in the fix were indicted by the first commissioner of baseball, Judge Kenesaw Mountain Landis, who was probably already bitter about getting stuck with a name like that.

So, far be it from me to condone Lance Armstrong's behavior, even though I, personally, am flawless, perfect, and staggeringly humble. I'm just saying that Lance is hardly the first blot on our collective American sports history, even though he singlehandedly took more drugs than a '69 Grateful Dead tour. Witness:

- Pete Rose, who regularly bet on ball games, unlike the other 300 million American sports fans, who regularly bet on ball games
- Barry Bonds, Marion Jones, Roger Clemens: these are just a few of the other athletes also accused of gobbling drugs that one normally associates with horses, circus animals, and Rolling Stones' guitarists

- Former Mets outfielder, Lenny "Nails" Dykstra, who stole cars during the off season, and who pleaded "not guilty" to exposing himself to women he met on Craigslist

- OJ Simpson, who, after being chased on a Los Angeles freeway at breakneck speeds of up to ten miles an hour, was arrested for impersonating a South Florida retiree

- Wilt Chamberlain, who allegedly had sex with the entire state of Michigan, but not on Craigslist

- Tiger Woods, who murdered his own career and then filed for divorce, claiming "irreconcilable differences in actual mileage" after his wife killed his car

- Tonya Harding, who tried to turn professional ice skating into a World Wrestling Federation cage match

- How the heck do you expose yourself on Craigslist, anyway? Somebody should look into this.

- Former Atlanta Falcon star, Michael Vick, who made dogs fight in front of an audience, as if the dogs were startlingly obese, double-branched relatives from a trailer park appearing on *"Jerry Springer"*

- LA Laker Kobe Bryant, who, inexplicably, was named after an expensive Japanese steak

- And Brett Favre, guilty of aggravated aggravation for telling everybody his name is pronounced "Farve"

But getting back to Te'o and his extremely thin girlfriend - I'm sure he'll be fine not having her not around; in fact, he's probably better off on his own. After all, imagine going through life in the company of a partner who's dealing with, shall we say, serious existence issues:

- Hey, Coach, can you get my girlfriend a ticket to the game? Just a ticket - she don't need a seat.
- No, two. Table for *two*. Right. No, *two! TWO!*
- Dude. When you said the "little" missus, I had no idea.
- I now pronounce you man and wi...hey! Where'd she go?
- Honey, look at all those wedding gifts that aren't really there!
- Yes, Officer, I understand it's the two-or-more-passenger lane. See, my wife is n...
- Listen, honey - they're playing our song! "Just the one of us..."
- Sure, we had a fight. But I can't believe how she treats me. She don't call; she don't write; she don't exist...

~-~-~-~-~-~

Oh, and here's some breaking news: During his tell-all interview on the Oprah Biking Safety Helmet channel, Lance Armstrong updated his weekly status, setting it back to "I was lying." But inside sources say he could be lying.

I am not good enough to make this stuff up.

This Just In!

America's news media. Because sometimes the facts just aren't enough!

<>~<>~~~~~~~~~~<>~<>~~~~~~~~~~<>~<>

CNN was the worst. But not by much.

No, not by much at all. As the American media rushed to out-scoop each other during Boston's cheetah-paced manhunt, their ratings-greedy race to the bottom was fierce.

But at the end of the day, CNN took home the dishonors.

To be fair, MSNBC's week had already gotten off to a rough start. Chris Matthews, MSNBC's star skull midget, was still recovering from other uncomfortable news: not only had a naughty lunatic mailed Ricin to Barack Obama, Matthews' personal hearth god; but the lunatic turned out to be a *Democrat* lunatic ... *and* an Elvis impersonator.

So when Chris and his tingly leg learned that the Boston bombers were *not*, in fact, white Republican heterosexuals, the distraught, already unstable MSNBC hair helmet could barely finish his imported free-range yak-milk yogurt and his bran muffin with the "I Heart Barack" fat-free icing.

FoxNews also chimed in from Boston, about every eighteen seconds, to keep viewers apprised of any historically-significant breaking news. For example, one of their rotating Foxes broke a story that ... now hold on to something ... the suspects may had attended the same high school as Matt Damon and Ben Affleck.

(Editor's Note: we missed the next few hours of news coverage, because at this point we reflexively rifled our coffee cup through our television screen. Our bad.)

After we returned from the TV store, Geraldo Rivera, FoxNews' pet liberal, had wriggled his way on-camera to do what he does best: inject himself into every story and make like he's in danger. He and his mustache, which has a common-law wife and its own passport, were busily regaling viewers with details about the time he'd been shot at in the Balkans (while attending high school with Ben Affleck), and the time he'd been shot at in Aruba (while playing strip body surfing with Matt Damon).

For their part, the "mainstream" news media performed about as you would expect. ("mainstream" being ABC, CBS, and their parent company, the White House Press Office. NBC no longer even *pretends* that they're reporting any actual facts anymore.) Team Mainstream kept us in the know during the week, in case there were any critical changes in the President's golf schedule, or his wife ran into any pesky vacation overlaps.

But despite these journalistic challenges, CNN tenaciously held on to their low standards, and as the manhunt unfolded, they managed to serve up some of the dumbest, most inaccurate reporting ever nearly fact-checked. At various times during the week, CNN broke these headlines from Boston:

- the bombers had been wounded
- the bombers had been surrounded, but then escaped
- the bombers had wounded Geraldo Rivera
- the bombers had won the Powerball lottery
- once, while winning the lottery, Geraldo had been shot at
- the bombers were, in fact, Matt Damon and Ben Affleck

Not to be out-alleged, crack MSNBC reporters filed their own front-pagers:

- the bombers had been wounded
- the bombers had wounded each other
- the bombers had been wounded by white Republican heterosexuals
- one of the bombers was an Elvis impersonator
- the bombers had been killed, but had recovered
- Barack Obama had captured the bombers, resuscitated Elvis, and solved *pi*

But then, on Wednesday, CNN simply lost control. They were breaking in with breaking news that didn't even comply with our known laws of physics:

- the bombers had been apprehended, but then they vanished
- they'd been abducted by extraterrestrial Elvis impersonators

- they'd committed suicide during an "Al Gore's Best Speeches" marathon on C-SPAN
- they agreed to speak at each other's funeral
- but then they hijacked the hearse and took off for Disney World
- they'd defeated the Bruins
- they had married each other, divorced and then remarried a third bomber, leading to an ugly custody battle over a pressure cooker and a set of commemorative Chechnyan railroad plates, and celebrity attorney Gloria Allred was representing the railroad

And then, later that evening, after subjecting us to that bath of bilge, CNN had the gall to issue a stern editorial, condemning news sources who rush to publish.

The resulting irony cloud was so immense, it caused a partial eclipse over Atlanta.

So. Now that we're clear to dispense with any semblance of truth, fact-checking, or journalistic integrity, let's recap some of last week's lowlights. Let's sift through the "chasing the bomber" news coverage...the reportage we all heard (or might as well have heard) from a ratings-craving American news media determined to be the first to deliver the news...even when there isn't any:

~-~-~-~-~-~

"This just in: we're now hearing that the suspect has eluded all 9,000 armed officers, and Dog the Bounty Hunter, despite the fugitive's wearing a bright yellow "I Heart Chechnya" windbreaker and lugging a Costco pallet of militarized bamboo steamers."

~-~-~-~-~-~-~

"This just in: according to our sources, the 9,000 pursuing officers fired so many rounds that they ran out of ammo and had to go borrow some bullets from the steno pool at Social Security."

~-~-~-~-~-~-~

"This just in: a troubled Harvard undergrad has been arrested for attempting to hold up a Cambridge bank with a crock pot bomb."

~-~-~-~-~-~-~

"By our estimate, the fugitive has now been shot at about 464,000 times, and the FBI is reporting that he's still alive. As the expression goes, 'You know, I don't believe I'd 'a told that.'"

~-~-~-~-~-~-~

Tonight on MSNBC: Chris Matthews notes that history is filled with white Republican heterosexuals, and history is filled with violence. We're just sayin'.

~-~-~-~-~-~-~

"This is Rank Macintosh, reporting for Channel 5 News. We're just learning that the suspect may be hiding in a nearby suburban neighborhood. For an update, let's go to our Nearby Suburban Neighborhood expert, Punta Hammurabi. Punta, whaddaya got?"

"Thanks, Rank. What we know right now is that it's a neighborhood. A residential neighborhood."

"Hmm. A *residential* neighborhood, eh? As opposed to a *what* neighb..."

"Excuse me, Rankster."

"Geraldo, we're on the air here! And don't call me 'Rankster.' Go ahead, Punta."

"To clarify, it's a neighborhood. A family-oriented area. Back to you, Rank."

"Folks, you heard it here first. I'm Rank Macintosh. And now we turn to ou..."

"Hey, Rank. Rankeroostie."

"*What?!?* Geraldo, for *Pete's sake*! What is it?"

"This reminds me of the time I was in a neighborhood in Belfast, and was shot at while cov..."

~-~-~-~-~-~

"This just in: after an intensive, house-to-house search in a tony Watertown neighborhood, there's still no sign of the suspect, but police did bust two undocumented Elvis impersonators, five meth labs, and an group of 12-year-olds running an email scam involving a money-laundering Nigerian prince."

~-~-~-~-~-~

Tonight on MSNBC: In an inspiring show of solidarity, the President boldly postponed a tee time, and First Lady Michelle Obama had her credit limit increased at Lord & Taylor.

~-~-~-~-~-~

"This just in: a disgruntled Red Sox fan has been arrested at Logan International for threatening to hijack a flight, and brandishing a Dutch oven."

~-~-~-~-~-~

Police have received a tip that the suspect is hiding under a boat tarp in somebody's backyard. That's right, folks: hiding, in a boat, on dry land, in a city called Watertown. In an unrelated story, Channel 5 News is running this on-screen headline: AUTHORITIES FLOOD NEIGHBORHOOD.

~-~-~-~-~-~

"This just in: as the Boston police closed in on the boat where the second bomber was hiding, they were forced to pull back when celebrity attorney Gloria Allred rappelled down from a chopper and offered to represent the perp, and the tarp."

~-~-~-~-~-~

Oh good. Geraldo Rivera is back on-camera. Any minute now, he'll be recalling the time he was forced to hide in a boat, high in the Hindu Kush. I don't know if anybody shot him in the Kush. But I might.

~-~-~-~-~-~-~

"This just in: in a brilliant tactical move, Boston police have called in Biff Tolleson, a recreational boat salesman. Biff will attempt to get the fugitive out of the boat by convincing him to switch to a Bayliner."

~-~-~-~-~-~-~

Tonight on MSNBC: Chris Matthews asks - did white Republican heterosexuals sink the *Titanic*?

~-~-~-~-~-~-~

"This just in: the second bomber has been captured, and is now being rushed by Boston Bruins fans to the nearest hospital, somewhere in rural Wyoming."

~-~-~-~-~-~-~

And a collective cheer went up across the nation, followed by a huge sigh of relief, as exhausted Americans let the news sink in: CNN's news coverage was over.

S*M*A*S*H

Welcome to the 38th Parallel...universe!

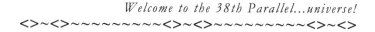

Let's play a game. Basically, it's a 'fact or fiction' quiz involving that zany Pacific Rim fun park, North Korea. I call it "Global Thermonuclear War and the Chia Pet."

I have the easy part. For the next few minutes, I'm going to write stuff about North Korea, and some of the stuff, I'm just gonna make up.

Yours is the tough job. You have to figure out which bits are true and which aren't. And if you're familiar with the madcap antics of North Korea's Fearless Leader and his fun-loving forebears, you know that picking out the true bits is gonna get a bit tricky.

Ready? Good luck!

~~-~~-~~-~~

Korea is thought to be one of the oldest countries on Earth, with signs of population since the Lower Paleolithic (literal translation: 'un-tanned lithics'). In fact, the area we now call Korea has been inhabited for 400,003 years.

"Get out," you skeptics out there may be skepticizing. "400,003? What do you mean, *three?*"

Yes. 400,003 years. I have this on good authority, because when a friend of mine visited Korea, her tour guide said Korea had been inhabited for 400,000 years, and the tour was three years ago.

(I told you this was gonna be tricky...)

However, despite all those SPF30-obsessed lithics, things in Korea got off to a slow start. In fact, it wasn't until the year 1000 BC that the first Korean pottery turned up. So not much happened for the first 399,007 years (yes, seven). In terms of getting anything productive done, protean Korea was a lot like the US Congress.

Finally, in 2333 BC, the ancient Korean kingdom of Gojoseon (literal translation: 'Samsung') was established by Dangun Wanggeom (literal translation: 'Steve'). Dangun claimed to be descended from heaven (literal translation: 'ego the size of Godzilla'); however, he needn't have rushed down here; after all, he had some 1300 years to kill before anybody even invented pottery. Thankfully for Dangun, though, somebody invented soju. (literal translation: 'Bud Lite')

According to legends, Dangun was out clubbing one night when, depending on which legend you read, one of two things happened: either he ran into a tiger and a bear that could talk, or else he'd invented the DUI. Legend says the two misguided animals petitioned Dangun to turn them into humans (they didn't know any better, because '*People*' magazine hadn't been invented yet). Dangun responded rather cryptically: he gave the tiger and the bear twenty cloves of garlic and a bundle of mugwort, and told them to avoid sunlight for 100 days (see 'un-tanned lithics'). After a few days of mugwort, the tiger gave up, bounded off, and ate a yak. But the bear persevered and became a woman who wore lots of turquoise, enrolled in a pottery class, and demanded free contraception.

(I told you this was gonna be tricky...)

Then, to the bear's great surprise, some 5000 years passed, which is the kind of thing that can happen when you're a mythical shape-shifting bear in some guy's humor column. Fast-forward to 1392 AD, when the Joseon Dynasty was established by an up-and-coming general who, with a straight face, called himself Yi Seong-gye. General Yi built a famous Korean palace, which he named Gyeongbokgung. (literal translation: 'About Four Billion Points in Scrabble')

Naval factoid: In 1598, another Yi, Admiral Yi Sun-sin, invented something called the turtle ship, a maritime nightmare which struck fear in the hearts of navies everywhere, particularly navies with ships modeled after small insects, or pond algae.

Not surprisingly then, over the millennia, the Korean peninsula has been marauded by most everyone except France: brutally invasive forces like China, Japan, Russia, Mongolia, Detroit, Barbra Streisand, and Samsung. Even the United Kingdom occupied tiny Geomun Island in 1885, but left almost immediately, possibly due to the British navy having no at-hand anti-turtle-ship tactics. (Hearing this news, France immediately surrendered to a Belgian tortoise.)

Finally, in 1919, the local population decided to get involved, since they'd already, like, invented pottery and stuff. Independence rallies broke out on 1 March 1919, and in one of those classically inscrutable Far Eastern moments, the uprising was dubbed 'the March 1st Movement.'

(I told you this was gonna, you know...)

In 1948, Kim il-Sung founded the modern nation of North Korea, became Prime Minister, and instituted his own variant of communism, which revolved around pottery co-ops, some kind of seasoned cabbage, and state-owned turtles.

Two years later, Korea was invaded by a movie starring Elliot Gould and Donald Sutherland; then invaded again by a TV show starring Alan Alda and a staggeringly unattractive woman named Jamie Farr (no relation to the bear).

Network factoid: Sutherland's son, Keister, would later star in a TV show called '*24*,' so named for the number of times each week that Keister's character would grab his cell phone and shout, "Chloe, send it now!"

Kim il-Sung is best known for his 1994 nuclear weapons talks with erstwhile US President Jimmy Carter, a world-changing summit during which both leaders complimented each other's teeth.

Following Kim il-Sung's death later that year (ruled a coincidence; however, Carter's teeth were briefly detained for questioning), the first Kim was succeeded by a string of Kims, including Kim Jong-il, Kim Chi, Kim Novak, Kim Basinger, and Korea's current Fearless Leader, Kim Jong Dongi Kong.

You're probably familiar with Kim Jong Dongi Kong and his country's current attempts to successfully launch WMD-type missiles, which are North Korea's chief export, if you don't count ursine-shaped anti-misogynist pottery. Their latest launch attempt stayed aloft for nearly 90 seconds before it fragmented and drowned in the Yellow Sea, taking out a turtle ship and two vacationing shrimp. In response to the launch, Iran immediately placed an order for two dozen missiles, and shrimp fried rice, while Ron Paul demanded we withdraw our troops from Red Lobster.

But for pure entertainment value, no Kim could touch Dongi Kong's dad, Kim Jong-il.

Kim Jong-il was - how can we put this delicately ... let's see ... remember that guy in '*One Flew Over the Cuckoo's Nest*' who, day after day after day, just waltzed around the ward with himself? Imagine *that* guy, but in a military green leisure suit and a Chia Pet hat. *That's* Kim Jong-il. I mean the man was his own magical mystery tour. First, the hair. His head looked like it was being attacked by a bear-fur-covered bamboo steamer. He wore oversized glasses so outlandish they would embarrass Elton John. Overly sensitive about his diminutive height, he wore platform shoes that would make a pole dancer drool.

Circa 1970 pimp shoes - always a good choice with military green leisure suits.

Kim Jong-il spent over $700,000 a year on cognac, according to family sources (Ma Jong). Reportedly, he never used the toilet, and he could levitate on demand. He was also immortal, which, coupled with the cognac, is a long time to not go to the bathroom.

To conclude our game, let's quickly calibrate your 'Kim' quotient, shall we?

According to Kim's official biography, what was unusual about his birth?
a)   A new star appeared in the sky
b)   The OB/GYN administered a cognac IV
c)   The OB/GYN forgot the cognac, and was executed
d)   At birth, he was as tall as he would ever get

What was Kim's traditional title?
a)   Dear Leader
b)   Dear Abby
c)   Steve
d)   Punkin Butt

What ceremonial post does Kim still hold, despite being dead?
a)   President for Eternity
b)   Secretary General for Eternity
c)   All-Seeing Deity of Stuff That Can Be All-Seen From A Height of, Say, 40 Inches, Give or Take
d)   Bladder Master

Based on some reports, Kim once studied in which maritime location?
a)   The Isle of Malta
b)   The Isle of Coney
c)   Fantasy Island
d)   Atlantis

How tall is Kim?
a)   5 foot 3
b)   3 foot 5
c)   He's actually 6 foot 8, but due to an humble respect for others, he stoops in public
d)   What, *now?*

According to North Korea's news agency, what record did Kim set during his first-ever round of golf?
a)   He scored eleven holes-in-one
b)   He scored eleven holes-in-one, on the front nine
c)   He had six caddies executed
d)   At the turn, he consumed $61,000 worth of Hennessy

What gift did US Secretary of State Madeleine Albright give Kim when she visited in 2000?
a)   A basketball signed by Michael Jordan
b)   A miniature golf scorecard signed by Billy Barty
c)   Michael Jordan
d)   Bill Clinton's Singapore rolodex

In 2001, Kim Jong-il's eldest son, Kim Jong-nam, embarrassed the entire nation. How?
a)   He was arrested with a false passport at Tokyo's airport
b)   During a heated game of Scrabble, he played the word AA

c) At Gyeongbokgung Palace, he tore that 'Do Not Remove' tag off a mattress

d) He was spotted at a club doing soju shooters with Britney Spears

According to a diplomatic source, what favorite thing did Kim have flown in regularly?

a) Live lobsters

b) Crates of cognac and pallets of 'Depends'

c) Randy Newman's 'Little Criminals' album with the song 'Short People' removed

d) Britney Spears

~~-~~-~~-~~

So, that's where we stand. That's the Korean situation in a nuthou ... er, nutshell. Now, I guess, it's up to the new Kim to write the next chapter. Will he take the reins, or will he barter with wistful bears? Will he grow into his global responsibilities, or will he out-odd his old man?

Most importantly - will Fearless Leader get to go to the bathroom?

Rise of the Guilt-Shifters

Rogue mid-level minions - the new "it's George Bush's fault"

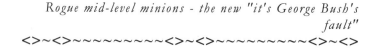

Carly knew she had a problem when her cellphone committed suicide.

The diagnosis was easy: shame. Somebody else's phone told Carly's phone that they were all being tapped - and not just by the Justice Department, but by several dozen government agencies; among them, the NSA, the CIA, the BLT, the LBJ, the MSNBC, the OB/GYN, and on, and on, and on:

- the Department of Education
- the Department of Reeducation
- the Department of Border Security, Paul Bunyan & Other Myths
- the Departments of Interior, Exterior, Posterior, Bull Terrier, and Border Security Terrier
- the Department of Oversized Cola Management
- the Department of Competitive Long Distance Calling Plans
- the Compartment Department
- the Deportment Department

- the Compliance Department In Charge Of Those 'Do Not Remove' Tags You Always See On New Mattresses
- the Agency for Social Media Monitoring & Acronym Analysis LOL
- the Bureau of Angry Birds

And so, burdened with all that digital ignominy, Carly figures the despondent device just took the easy way out.

The stupid smartphone killed itself.

Cellular Suicide. Kamikaze Keyboard. Autodial Asphyxia.

There's an app for that.

But this little cyber-tragedy serves as a reminder of just how psychotic things have gotten in American politics - even the *electronics* are fed up.

I think we're witnessing the evolution of a new life form (well, new *low*-life form): the Guilt-Shifter. I mean, look at our current crop of career pols inside the beltway: these tap-dancing truth-twisters make Richard Nixon look like Honest Abe on a sodium pentothal binge.

To make the point, let's just take a quick look at a few random *non mea culpa* samplings from recent headlines, presented in no particular disorder:

- One of the forty or fifty scandals currently soiling the White House involves the IRS's illegal targeting of Obama's political enemies. First, the IRS admitted it. Then they apologized for it. Next, they denied doing what they'd already admitted to and apologized for. Then they blamed what they said hadn't happened on rogue mid-level minions in an obscure Rust Belt office. Finally, during the season finale, J.R. woke up Obama and they all realized it was just a dream, brought on by extended exposure to Al Gore speeches.

- The Pentagon has admitted to buying military parts from China. However, since China stole the plans for the parts from US companies anyway, the Pentagon positioned the maneuver as a cost-cutting victory.

- According to a recent poll, 83% of American adults agree that the US Government has a spending problem...which means that 14% of those polled *don't think there's a problem.* Of the other adults in the sample, 2% looked confused and kept saying "Que?" and the remaining 1% stole the interviewer's microphone.

- Across the globe, political tensions grew as the world learned that tough-as-nails Secretary of State Hillary Clinton had resigned, and had been replaced by a woman.

- In Maryland, a seven-year-old student was suspended for biting a Pop-Tart into the shape of a gun. Fortunately, the snack misfired and no one was killed; however, the tart-toting truant did stage an impromptu anti-nap protest, wounding three crayons and holding several graham crackers hostage. Fortunately, the kid was subdued, just before story time, by a heavily-armed Social Security Administration SWAT team wearing full-body armor and diabetic socks.

- Once somebody finally told President Obama about the cellphone-tapping scandal, the President rushed to a teleprompter to deny it, and then to downplay it, and then to remind everybody to quit whining 'cause he'd given them the cellphones in the first place. After reading his lines, the President took a few questions from reporters, but eventually he gave the questions back.

- Eric "I Have No Idea" Holder, America's Top Cop, has been the subject of so many ongoing investigations that he's managed to set a dubious record: for the first time in history, the man at the *top* of the FBI's "Most Wanted" list is also the man who *compiles* the FBI's "Most Wanted" list.

- During a speech to the "Texas Caucus of Whiny Rich Females Who Act Like Victims," Congressdroid Sheila Jackson-Lee made the angry accusation that the Moon is white due to rampant racism. As usual, SJ-L showed up draped in some kind of painter's drop-cloth, and sporting that odd loaf of braided Greek bread on her head.

- In a rare free moment in-between indictments, HHS Maven Kathleen Sebelius altered a paragraph on page 24,921,855 of the ObamaCare manual's foreword, resulting in free life-long health care for everyone in Central America, including livestock, and left-leaning Panther Gods, and rogue mid-level minions.

- Senator Orrin Hatch said he supports a No-Fly Zone in Syria. The nearly Reverend Al Sharpton charged the conservative Senator with rampant racism, pointing out that flies are black. Senate Democrats promptly countered with a bill providing ObamaCare benefits to gnats and no-see-ums.

- America began coming to terms with some hard news: there's a strong chance that a nasty, venom-filled female will run for President in 2016; we just don't know if it'll be Hillary Clinton or some other career trixie, like Sheila Jackson-Lee, or John Kerry.

- While channel-surfing, President Obama finally learned that, for the first time in 600 years, a Pope had resigned. The President quickly grabbed a teleprompter, read a bunch of papal bull, and pardoned the 16th Century. After reading his lines, the President took a few questions from reporters, but keeping the spirit of the day, he lied in Latin.

- As part of a Congressional hearing into, um, I think it was Scandal 74-B, America's director of intelligence acted like he didn't have any. When asked if his agency had been spying on Americans, the hairless NSA head feverishly scratched his hairless NSA head, scowled, and then uttered this jaw-dropping response: "Not wittingly." Then, later in the week, he defended his testimony by saying he had responded in the "least untruthful" way.

- Whoa. You gotta admire people who can spew bilge like that *and* keep a straight face.

- At a recent white House news conference, three rogue mid-level minions manning Obama's twin teleprompters were seriously wounded when John Kerry lobbed two of his fake medals across the Rose Garden. Since the rogue mid-level minions were wounded "in action," Kerry applied for another Purple Heart. After reading his lines, the President took a few questions from reporters, and then redistributed them to other less fortunate reporters who didn't have as many questions.

- Meanwhile, NOAA, our taxpayer-funded national weather service, is buying up the same automatic weapons and ammo-by-the-bus-load that Congress is trying to keep *us* from owning. To be fair, though, it *has* been a brutal season for tornados, and hurricane season is upon us. Maybe the weather spotters' plan is to get the storms classified as political enemies, and shoot the storms.

- Late one Tuesday, Congress slipped into Washington in-between vacations and demanded the IRS hand over, by a certain date, a bunch of hopefully-incriminating documents. Those light-hearted, live-and-let-live jokesters at the IRS missed the deadline.

- Seriously. *The IRS missed a filing deadline.*

- Now *that's* funny.

See? It's the dawn of a new age. It's the rise of the Guilt-Shifters.

And everywhere you go, you bump into yet another numbed human who's bought into this dystopian blamelessness. (The new-and-improved Guilt-Shifter! Order now! A No-Fault Life awaits you!) So now it's left to the electronics to learn how to cope. I suggest you contact an online, off-shore pharmacy and get your smartphone a scrip for Xanax.

There's an app for that.

The Pope, the Dope, & the Misanthrope

Move over, Axis of Evil. Make way for the Axis of Stupid.

<>~<>~~~~~~~~~~<>~<>~~~~~~~~~~<>~<>

Ever wish you were rich and famous? Ever wish you could command millions of citizens, and dress funny on purpose? Well, be careful what you wish for. So far this year, one dictator died, another one befriended a metallic mutant, and a Pope quit.

It's turning out to be a tough year if you're infallible.

~_~_~_~_~_~

For starters, Dennis Rodman just got back from North Korea, and if that sentence doesn't confuse you, you're lying.

It's true, though. Dennis Rodman, former NBA tattoo museum and current runway model for *Brides* magazine, just returned from a chatty in-country visit with North Korea's leader, Kim Novak. (young Kim inherited the country from his father, Kim Basinger - along with a cellar-full of top-shelf Scotch, a great big army, and a really bad barber)

The international story was intensely scrutinized by crack geopolitical analysts at America's most astute institutions - respected think tanks like the *National Enquirer*, the cast of *The View*, and Secretary of State John Kerry's favorite source of intel, the foreign desk at *Giant Mutant Alien Babies Born During Soap Operas To Dieting Lottery Winners Weekly*.

Shrewd observers think young Kim's invite may have been prompted by Dennis' impressive collection of metallic face piercings. It could be that Dear Leader Take Two planned to strip-mine Rodman's head for nuclear fuel rods.

Overall, Rodman seemed to enjoy the visit, despite the traveling inconvenience of having to stow his speared face with the checked baggage. During his stay in North Korea, Dennis even dabbled in affairs of state, reportedly offering this olive branch to Tiny Kim: "You like basketball. Obama likes basketball. Let's start there."

Uncanny. It's like Kissinger, but with a poleaxe in his nose.

Decades from now, our children will proudly recall this historic moment - the beginning of a new American foreign policy: Double-Dribble Diplomacy.

Or not. We're now hearing that, after Rodman left, Kim eased back into Standard Psycho. The little Kimlet stood on several thick phone books, grabbed a mike, and threatened to cancel the 1953 cease-fire that ended the Korean War.

And our world can barely grasp the horrible realities that might be unleashed by such an action: a remake of M*A*S*H, starring Dennis Rodman as Corporal Klinger.

~.~.~.~.~.~

In news closer to home: at the Vatican, Pope Benedict XVI has turned in his keys, citing a growing dislike with being a Roman numeral, and lower back pains from having to walk around all day wearing that hat. (The ex-Pope is not really named Benedict XVI, of course. His *real* name is Fred XVI.)

This marks the first time in over DC years that a Pope has resigned, and the *only* time a Pope has quit without being forced out by a scandal, or by large, meddling Italian families named Borgia, Medici, or Soprano. (By the way, DC is Roman numeralese for 600, in case you're the leader of North Korea, or the Mayor of New York.)

Six hundred years. Imagine that. The last time a Pope hung up his post-hole-digger hat, America hadn't even been *discovered* yet, much less purchased by the Chinese. Six hundred years ago, Joan of Arc was still alive, and dating Strom Thurmond. Heck, six hundred Roman numerals ago was so far back, golf balls had just been invented, though to this day nobody knows why.

Around MCDXI or so, somebody invented the trigger; sadly, though, it would be over LX years before anybody invented a rifle. However, in a preemptive strike, a meddlesome medieval twit named Senator Dianne Feinstein sponsored the Assault Triggers ban of 1412, a law which made it illegal IV trigger owners II point a finger and say "bang! bang!" within L feet of a school zone.

In the mid-MCDs, a master printer named Johann Gutenberg invented Amazon.com, but he was immediately beheaded by a brigand named Barnes the Noble. And the year MCDLXXXVI saw the first-ever copyright, granted to an up-and-coming young author named King Stephen XIII (writing as Sir Richard of Bachman) for his suspenseful novel *Ye Olde Shining.*

(In 1491, Amazon.com was optioned by Spain's Queen Isabella, as part of a hostile takeover that became known as the Spanish Acquisition. A *seriously* hostile takeover.)

Around the end of the century, Leonardo da Vinci invented the parachute, just in case anybody ever invented planes, or in case the then-current Pontiff, Pope MC Hammer, ever ran out of chinos. A few years later, the Scots invented Scotch - probably to atone for having invented golf. And then, barely six months after the Italians had discovered Scotch, da Vinci released something he called his "Vitruvian Man," a drawing of a naked guy with four arms, four legs, and Bette Midler's hair.

Barely six months. That's all I'm saying.

A few weeks later, during a "da Vinci is da Bomb" carnival in Venice, Pope MC I somehow got into the Scotch, strapped on one of da Vinci's chutes, and Europe witnessed its first parasailing accident. And that, children, is where we get the expression "Pope on a Rope."

(Fortunately for music-lovers everywhere, Pope Hammer survived the accident and went on to pen that perennial monastery favorite, "Verily Canst Thou Not Touch This.")

Actually, at one point about 600 years ago, there were *three* Pontiffs running around Europe, simultaneously pontificrastinating at anything that moved. For a short while, it was as if picking a Pope was some bizarre, high-stakes game of Vatican Hold 'Em. In Rome, the Vatican opened the betting with an Urban VI. Team France pursed its lips, rhythmically tapped a blue chip for a few seconds, and then barked, "I'll see your Urban VI and raise you one Clement VII." Cardinals from Pisa then bluffed with an Alexander V, hoping to fill an inside straight from Gregory XII to John XXIII.

Finally, Alexander died, Gregory resigned, John was deposed, and the Council of Constance elected a new pope, Martin V. But it turned out that nobody anywhere was willing to seriously heed the pronouncements of a pope named 'Martin.' It would've been like being among 150,000 adoring celebrants in St. Peter's Square when the trumpet sounds, the little louvered doors open, and out on to the balcony, steps...

Pope Billy.

So Il Papa Martin was out before he ever even got fitted for a Kevlar golf cart, though he did receive some nice parting gifts. The Swiss guard comped his lunch, validated his parking, and Martin was escorted out the side gate.

The next day, the cardinals installed as their new pope a lovely gentlemen, Clement IX, who worked out swimmingly, was adored by the faithful, and became the inspiration for that catchy 3/4 ditty, "O my darlin,' O my darlin,' O my darlin,' Clement Nine."

~-~-~-~-~-~

Meanwhile, down in Venezuela, a great man has probably died. Somewhere.

Unfortunately, *that* guy didn't make the news.

What *did* make the headlines was the death of Hugo Chavez, Venezuela's jowly dictator and Sean Penn's personal write-in candidate for Pope of Hollywood. Chavez, 58, died last month from extended exposure to Cuban health care, after the CIA speared him with a super-secret cancer dart.

According to Chavez supporters, El Mico Mandante legitimately won several elections during his tenure, especially once you convince local poll-watchers that 115% of the vote qualifies as 'legitimate.' Conversely, Chavez detractors like to point out that El Commandante 'won' in ways that would likely have spawned outrage in the US, if *American Idol* wasn't on.

That 'yanqui cancer dart' comment was attributed to Hugo's hand-picked successor, Nicolas Maduro, by all reports a solid, rational leader who, by comparison, makes Grigori Rasputin look like Barbara Bush. After the swearing-in ceremony, Maduro appeared on the country's state-run TV channel, the 7-watt powerhouse, WKGB, wearing a Fidel-style cap, a camo push-up bra, and parachute pants.

And there, as the entire country watched, Maduro admitted that Chavez may have died from injuries sustained when he tripped over that big red line at the equator. Next, Maduro issued his first Presidential fiat, ordering all Venezuelan men to change their names to Simon Bolivar, and all women to change theirs to Dennis Rodman.

And then, on national TV, the new leader of Venezuela broke into a medley of show tunes from 'Cats.'

Inside sources say that Dennis Rodman was crushed by the news of Hugo's passing, and that Rodman has canceled taping for an upcoming HGTV special, where his face had been invited to guest-star as a fuse box.

~-~-~-~-~-~

Just another week on Planet Earth.

Be careful what you wish for.

Sergeant Schultz Pleads the Fifth

Once you can fake sincerity, the rest is easy.

<>~<>~~~~~~~~~~<>~<>~~~~~~~~~~<>~<>

"I know nothing."

Remember that line? Once upon a time, *"I know nothing"* was the trademark alibi of Sergeant Schultz, that inept but lovable Nazi from the 1960s sitcom, *Hogan's Heroes.*

Nowadays, it's official White House policy.

Lately, it's been a tricky exercise, trying to keep up with the news oozing out of the Oval Office. Over the last few weeks, the pathologically bumbling White House has managed to make itself the tabloids' favorite filth, trumping even Trump, Beyoncé, and rumors of their alien zero-trans-fat love child (midwifed by Brad Pitt). Every dawn, a new allegation: if it's not a new scandal, it's a new cover-up of an earlier scandal. And all of it coordinated with the competence of Lucy and Ethel packaging chocolates.

This is mismanagement as defined in that obligatory "How To Don't" chapter they include in "How To" books. I've seen less fumbles in a Michael Vick game film marathon. And personnel are getting shuffled around from position to position so fast, you'd think you were watching the Vatican during a saltpeter shortage.

This is gross negligence of the worst kind. This is right up there with Hollywood approving funding for the movie *"Ishtar."*

And everybody, everywhere - regardless of which political party's "Please donate today!" mailings they throw away every week - *everybody* is saying, "What the heck happened?"

It's as though the entire inside-the-Beltway ecosystem was just a giant buffoon-filled balloon, and somebody pulled the plug - and now all the stupidity's streaming out.

And suddenly, as we all watched, everyone in the White House shaped-shifted into Sergeant Schultz.

Or think of it this way: imagine the current administration is a used car. You bought the thing in a hurry, late one November Tuesday, from some guy named Louie, and now the warranty has expired. Suddenly, nothing in the car works, and when you try to call Louie, you get a recording from some South Florida dance club called the Platinum Plus, inviting you to enjoy their lunch buffet.

The avalanche of asininity got so bad that Michelle Obama even decided to cancel her weekly jaunt to go get some Belgian waffles.

In Belgium.

Maybe we, the voting public, all aimed a bit high. Maybe we're all guilty of expecting a bit too much, given the raw materials we had to work with. Let's review:

- We have a President who's never run a staple remover, much less a State or a nation- heck, he's never even run a *fever* - but who, regardless, thinks he can oversee the largest hostile takeover of government since Hannibal.
- We have a Vice President whose sole résumé bullet is "takes the train to work," and whose entire skillset consists of two tools: cursing and malaprops. Remember: this is the guy who points out dead war heroes in the audience, who thought FDR had a TV, and who thinks "jobs" is a three-letter word. I mean, the man makes Yogi Berra look like Daniel Webster.
- We have an Attorney General who suffers from fraternity keg party-like blackouts, during which he recuses himself from ongoing investigations, and then can't recall doing it. (Nixon's burglars would've paid cash money for horse-traders like this.)
- We have a CIA that gets caught outfitting its spies with wigs so cheesy, Harpo Marx wouldn't wear them.
- We have a welfare system that expects the Treasury to pay for abortions, a Treasury Secretary who doesn't pay his taxes, and an tax agency that's about to open an OB/GYN clinic.
- We have a homeland security provider that doesn't, a space exploration agency that can't, and a border protection force that won't.

- And we have a White House press secretary who, to be honest, looks quite promising and should have a stellar career, once he reaches puberty.

So. Given the ingredients we agreed to buy, maybe we shouldn't pretend to be surprised when we're served "breaking news" meals like these:

- Earlier today, Jay "Spanky" Carney, White House Press Secretary and pending Cub Scout, was a half-hour late for a scheduled press briefing. A deputy assistant adjutant sub-secretary blamed the delay on Carney's having to put a Flintstones bandie on a boo-boo.
- During yesterday's hearings (Scandal 5J-3, Sub-scandal S9), Congressional leaders grilled some guy with a curled perm who either runs the IRS, or doesn't, or ran it last week, or will run it starting next week. He may or may not have responded to their questions, but his hair was fabulous.
- According to whistle-blowers, Obama's HHS Secretary, Kathleen "Cruella" Sebelius, may have gotten caught strong-arming private companies for "donations" (Scandal 11Z). Springing into damage control mode, the White House Office of Distractions and Shiny Objects announced that ObamaCare would now cover "post-existing conditions."
- Earlier today, Jay "Skippy" Carney, the White House Press Secretary and cabaña boy, set a new world's record in the Juvenile Obfuscation Olympics with his comment, "The president was not present when he made that decision."
- During today's Congressional hearings, the future temporary former acting co-ex-head of the IRS apologized for targeting political groups, while he denied targeting

political groups. The questioning was interrupted several times, due to the IRS chief's pants being on fire.

- After making everybody wait in the rain for twenty minutes, President Obama showed up ~~with a tourniquet~~ for a press conference and ~~read his lines~~ delivered an impassioned heart-felt speech about the ~~alleged~~ crimes committed by his IRS. Then he re-read script #723 (you know, the one where he's gonna hold everybody accountable), followed by that time-honored standard, "Bush's fault." For those of you keeping score at home, "Bush's fault" is script #441, just between #440 ("inheriting messes") and #442. ("pivoting like a laser on the economy")

- Overnight, tornadoes ripped across the state of Texas which, as everyone knows, is filled with gun-toting Bible owners. Jay "Baby Faust" Carney blamed the violent weather on sequestration.

- In a desperate attempt to stymie investigators, the White House flatly denied the existence of any "Benghazi-related" emails, and then released 95 of them. Security analysts combing over the emails determined that eleven contained jokes tweeted by George Takai, and another eighty-four were forwarded photos of a Grumpy Cat.

- According to sworn testimony before Congress, IRS agents were not, in fact, consciously picking on Obama's political enemies; rather, they all just happened to have been reading the same bedtime picture book, titled "Alice the Conservative Pachyderm Invites Billy Graham To a Tea Party."

- As the White House labored to manage the IRS' own version of Bill Clinton's "bimbo eruptions," questions continued to mount concerning the tax agency's upcoming czar-like role in everyone's health care. President Obama responded quickly: "If ... *IF* this alleged favoritism turns out to be true, and if the IRS *does* cause your death by intentionally replacing your Republican spleen with a loofah sponge, then make no mistake - at your funeral, I will sing six notes from an Al Green song." The White House immediately released this comforting assurance from the President, taped at an undisclosed location. Then he missed a putt.

- Late yesterday, Jay "Little Boy Blue State" Carney held an off-the-record briefing, during which he blamed the Benghazi affair on the fact that, decades earlier, CBS had cancelled M*A*S*H.

- At the end of a long week, President Obama called Britain's Prime Minister to offer his condolences, after the President learned that the Beatles had broken up. The President then turned to his White House guest, the leader of Turkey, and asked him, "So, how's it going in Constantinople?"

But, as in all things, there's a bright side. In the face of all this incompetence, let's be sure we take the time to give credit where credit is due. We have to give *some* "sense of humor" credit to ... *somebody* ... at the IRS.

Among all the driftwood, we learned this week that the IRS have their own inter-agency softball team. And the IRS softball team call themselves ... ready?

The Cheetahs.

Finals Week at Gitmo U

A job interview primer. No, not that kind of primer.
<>~<>~~~~~~~~~<>~<>~~~~~~~~~~<>~<>

I have good news and bad news. Here's the bad news: The Gitmo soccer league has disbanded. (I know, I know. It's a crushing blow, but stay strong. The feeling will pass.)

As it turns out, when putting together a rehab program for violently self-destructive behavior, cleats and knee pads don't cut it. The allure of team sports faded quickly for the more individually-minded detainees at the Guantanamo Bay Maximum Sports Facility For Terrorists Who Forgot To Light The Fuse In Their Underwear. So the "intramural" theory was scratched, behavioral sociologists hunkered down, scribbled for a while on white boards, and have now decided to have the "terrorist detainees" reclassified as "alternatively motivated students." And, as a result, American taxpayers are being asked to pony up so the "students" can rehabilitate their careers, refine their social etiquette skills, and attend classes like *How to Write a More Effective Résumé.*

The good news? The students still want to blow up their underwear. So at least they've not gotten demotivated.

Now, remember, this is classified information. Top-secret stuff. Gitmo internal details are matters of national security. So how did we get this scoop? We stood around outside the headquarters of MSNBC until somebody from the White House leaked the info.

We waited about eight minutes.

Here, then, are some excerpts from a Gitmo re-education brochure, entitled *My First Interview*. You'll discover that job hunting is much the same for everyone. And you may discover that we have much in common ... all except for that 'blow yourself up' part.

~-~-~-~-~-~

Welcome!

Welcome to Gitmo U, brought to you by the American taxpayer! We're glad you've elected to take a few moments off from your busy schedule of pacing and glaring sullenly!

Well, let's get started, shall we? Let's say you've been captured while trying to blow yourself up, you've completed Gitmo rehab, and now you have an interview for a mindless clerical job in suburban Indiana, where you'll sit in a cube, day after soul-numbing day, reviewing bitter, misspelled emails from disgruntled customers of an American company that makes personalized calendars with little pictures of Disney animals on the cover and clever pop-up event reminders like "Oh deer, is it ewe birthday?"

Why, it's a dream come true! So let's prepare ourselves, shall we?

The Phone Interview

Employers may use telephone interviews for various reasons:

1) As a tool to narrow the pool of applicants who will be invited for in-person interviews
2) As a way to minimize the expenses involved in interviewing out-of-town candidates
3) Because they are smug, self-important grimeballs who feed on false perceptions of power and like to waste your time by calling you from their car and then making comments like "Hold on, I have to park."

During the Phone Interview

1) Don't smoke, chew gum, eat, drink, or blow anything up.
2) Don't hum, chant, ululate, or refer to any personal hearth deities by name.
3) Keep a glass of water handy, in case you need to wet your mouth, or you inadvertently blow something up.
4) Give short, concise answers; however, avoid expressions like "well, duh" and "nyet."
5) Smiling during a phone call enhances the tone of your voice and helps project a positive image to the listener. So smile broadly, unless you're in the middle of a sanity evaluation. Note: if you take the call from a public phone, be aware that smiling and talking to people that aren't there may disturb the other passengers.

6) Remember: your goal is to set up a face-to-face interview, so don't forget to ask if it would be possible to meet in person. And be sure to congratulate them on their parking skills.

~.~.~.~.~.~.~

How to Dress for an Interview

1) Stick with tame, solid colors; a modest two-piece suit or business outfit, cleaned and pressed, will win the day. Avoid loud colors, tie-dyed shirts, spandex, ceremonial plumage and medieval weaponry.

2) Don't wear buttons bearing political slogans, or t-shirts stamped with clever conversation starters like 'I Heart Chaos' or 'Mao Lives.' This is not the time or place for flaunting causes, regardless of your commitment to solar-powered undersea windmills, universal access to repressed literature about the gender inequality facing grafted roses, or having humpback whales admitted to the U.N.

3) For today, put aside that spiked leather collar, and anything else that involves a leash.

4) Perfumes and Colognes: simply put, less is more. Remember, it's a nuance, not a marinade. The last thing you want to do is bust up in some poor interviewer's office wrapped in a fragrance force field that smells like Tripoli looks. Plus, you're walking into unknown territory, and you must take into account personal preferences, tastes, allergies, prevailing wind patterns - even personal histories! Your tastefully-applied eau du jour may be the very same scent worn by the interviewer's recently estranged ex-wife, who just ran off with his mistress' girlfriend and who,

before leaving, spitefully filled his air conditioning ductwork with irradiated shrimp carcasses. Also, keep in mind that different cultures embrace (or eschew) different scents. Don't assume that your potential employer is as fond as was your last boss of regional exotics like 'Low-Tide Harem' or 'Southern Essence of Northbound Pack Animal.'

5) Pantyhose: the question of whether women should wear pantyhose on a job interview always generates a lot of discussion, and the collective answer is an overwhelming *yes*. For those of you who might be in a correctional facility for armed robbery, we should point out that we only endorse wearing pantyhose on one's *legs*. (Pantyhose as ski mask is covered in our fine arts elective: "Archetypal Career Decisions: a *Raising Arizona* retrospective")

6) Tattoos and Body Piercings: far be it from us to judge, but look - if you've poked a bunch of holes in your own head, why should Human Resources assume you can be trusted with office supplies?

What Not to Wear at an Interview

1) Jeans, shorts, or short skirts
2) Jewelry that doubles as a roach clip, coke spoon, or igniter
3) Sneakers, flip-flops, or combustible shoe inserts
4) Very short fuses

~-~-~-~-~-~-~

Phrases to Avoid During an Interview

1) Yeah, yeah, yeah, whatever. Cut to the money.

2) That your daughter's picture? Whoa. Nice yams, Pops!

3) Skills? Well, at the very least, I could do what *you* do.

4) You're kidding, right? Long-term disability? Have you *seen* my résumé?

5) Show up *whe* ... Seriously? *Every week?*

6) Dude, could we wrap this up? I'm supposed to meet my parole officer in fifteen.

~-~-~-~-~-~

Rehearsing For Your Interview

An often overlooked interview tactic is one that can make all the difference - practice. Here are some examples of questions *you* may be asked - think about how *you* would answer them!

Q) Give an example of how you cope with difficult clients or co-workers.
A) I blow myself up.

Q) Tell me about how you have worked effectively under pressure.
A) I blew myself up.

Q) Do you consider yourself a good listener?
A) I blew myself up.

Q) Have you ever dealt with a company policy you weren't in agreement with? How?
A) I blew up the policy.

Q) Give an example of when you used logic to solve a problem.

A) Once, at a midnight showing of *The Rocky Horror Picture Show*, I challenged the claim that mathematics is an axiomatic deduction system, inferring rather that, due to its antecedent disjunction, it in fact lies somewhere between a modus tollens and modus ponens. Then I blew myself up.

Q) Give an example of how you worked as part of a functional team.

A) I blew myself up last.

Q) Have you ever not met your goals?

A) Never. But I have lowered my expectations.

Q) Give an example of a goal you didn't meet and how you handled it.

A) You're not listening.

~-~-~-~-~-~-~

Well, there you have it, citizens. Your tax dollars at work! I'm sure the bad guys will think twice now, once they realize that here in America, we will not falter, we will not rest, until those who wish to do us harm have a full-time job, with benefits and paid holidays.

And the 12-15 million Americans who are unemployed? No worries.

I know where they can get a *great* deal on cleats.

Hello! I Must Be Going.

Banter that only a brother could love. A Marx Brother.
<>~<>~~~~~~~~~~~<>~<>~~~~~~~~~~~<>~<>

I don't know if you looked in on the lone 2012 Vice Presidential debate, but it was something to see...especially if you're a fan of watching unbalanced people in positions of authority who look like the Cheshire Cat and act like the Joker.

And, c'mon - be honest. Who isn't a fan of that?

It wasn't so much a debate as it was a drive-by; fortunately, Paul Ryan, the national politics newcomer, managed to walk away from the accident.

Basically, Ryan got gang-debated.

Paul Ryan's demeanor was that of a younger man trying to be polite in the presence of his elders, albeit an elder who'd snagged the keys to the nurses' station and then spent the afternoon nipping at the nitrous oxide.

For his part, Joe Biden spent the evening giggling like Bram Stoker's Renfield at a spider buffet. And when he wasn't snickering, he was wailing at the skies like some long-suffering relative of George Costanza, or blinding the hapless audience with some horrid reflective device embedded in his mouth.

(Defense analysts have since confirmed that the child-frightening wall of white was either Biden's eight over-polished incisors, or else the Pentagon's Psy-Ops group was testing a new citizen-blinding weapon. As someone online put it, "Joe Biden's teeth were so white that they're voting for Mitt Romney.")

And when Joe wasn't using parts of his face as a lethal weapon, he was interrupting - or interrupting the moderator's interrupting.

At one point during the debate debacle - and this was a first in rhetorical history - Joe Biden actually interrupted himself.

The moderator, a gaunt lady named Martha, who has more ties to the Obama administration than the Indonesian Society for the Promotion of Canine-Flavored Hot Pockets, quickly proved to be out of her league. Oh, she managed the debate...in the same sense that Margaret Dumont used to 'manage' the Marx Brothers.

But I'll let you decide how it went. Here's the actual, minute-by-minute transcript of the debate.

As far as you know.

~-~-~-~-~-~-~~-~-~-~-~-~

Martha: Ladies and gentlemen, and Republicans, welcome to the first and only Vice-Presidential debate. My name is Martha, and I'll be your moderator tonight for this debate between former Senator and current Vice President Joe Biden, one of the finest people I know, and that shifty-looking guy next to him. I've been selec...

Biden: Hey, who ya gonna believe? HA HA HA HA HA.

Martha: Not yet, Joe.

Biden: Pick up the pace, Toots.

Martha: (unintelligible comment) I've been selected to moderate tonight's event due to my professional objectivity and my off-the-clock isolation from politics, as evidenced by the fact that Barack Obama was a guest at my wedding, Barack Obama appointed my husband to head the FCC, and I personally contributed to former Senator and current Vice President Joe Biden's fabulous dental work.

Biden: Thanks, babe. And hello to all my friends here in the great state of Florida.

Martha: West Virginia.

Biden: Whatever.

Ryan: Martha, may I say 'thank you' for agreeing to modera...

Martha: In a minute, Todd.

Ryan: It's Paul.

Martha: Whatever.

Biden: Let me tell you good folks something. I am six-foot eight, and that's a fact. That. Is. A. Fact.

Martha: In the interest of bipartisan fair play, we'll let that bizarre, baseless statement go completely unchallenged, which gives our audience some idea of what the evening's gonna be like. And with that, let's get started. Our first category is 'photographs of kittens buried under volcanic lava.'

Biden: HA HA HA HA HA HA HA HA HA HA.

Ryan: That's horrible. But I'm not sure I understand how that's relev...

Martha: Time's up, Todd. Your rebuttal, former Senator and Vice President Joe Biden?

Biden: My friend knows very well where I stand on the torched kitten issue. Why, just last week, a modified report suggested that my friend's budget will slash 800 millio...600 mi...1.7 trill...five dollars from milk subsidies for Kitty Welfare. *(raises both arms, apparently in supplication to the klieg lights)* What in the world were they thinking?

Ryan: I have to take issue with those numbers. Even the nonpartisan analysis by severa...

Martha: Time's up, Bill.

Ryan: Paul.

Martha: Whatever.

Biden: HA HA HA HA HA HA HA HA HA HA HA HA HA HA HA.

Ryan: Will you *please* let me say something?

Biden: I hardly think so.

Martha: (rim shot)

Ghost of Groucho Marx: Hey, that's *my* line!

Biden: Martha, I think I love you.

Martha: I don't think you'd love me if I were poor.

Biden: Well, I might, but I'd keep my mouth shut.

Ryan: (rim shot)

Groucho's Ghost: HEY!

Martha: We'll take a short break, and when we come back, I'll explain why I appear to have no bones in my face.

(Commercial)

Martha: Welcome back. Let's move now to a topi...

Biden: Ever been to a biker bar, Toots?

Martha: Not now, Joe.

Biden: HA HA HA HA.

Ryan: Does he always grin like that?

Martha: Mind your tone, rookie.

Biden: Besides, Syria is five times larger geographically than Libya.

Ryan: Huh?

Biden: That. Is. A. Fact.

Groucho: Hey, who ya gonna believe? Me or your own eyes?

Ryan: Look, with all due respe...

Martha: Anybody seen my cheeks?

Biden: I hope I'll get equal time.

Ryan: (muttering) I hope you get *hard* time.

Martha: Carl, I'm not gonna warn you again. One more remark like that, and I'll turn this debate right around!

Ryan: It's *not* Carl, it's *Todd!* No, I mean, *Paul!* It's *Paul!*

Groucho: What, you didn't like Todd?

Chico: (rim shot)

Martha: Let's move now to a topic on the minds of all voters: foreign affairs. And we'll begin this round with...uh...with the guy sitting on my right. Carl, is it?

Ryan: (sigh) Todd.

Martha: Whatever.

Groucho: Atta boy.

Biden: HA HA HA HA HA.

Martha: Carl, please list all of the world's leaders, alphabetically by height.

Ryan: Well, there's Abu Almat, and Adam Prkysnk, and Ari Pipi Ngobo, Bryn Enho...

Biden: HA HA HA HA HA HA!

Ryan: WHAT? What is so funny?

Biden: (giggling) He said 'pee pee.'

Groucho: I'm not getting any straight lines here.

Martha: Get out of the gutter, Todd.

Ryan: Yes, sir or ma'am.

Groucho: Atta boy.

Martha: Okay. Based on that stumbling response to a simple question about world leaders, I'm certain the entire American voting public realizes just how poorly this Todd guy would do, were he to assume the role of Vice President, especially a Vice President with semaphore-ready teeth and hair implants.

Biden: (giggling) He said 'pee pee.'

Chico: He's got a point, this teeth guy.

Biden: Those are my principles. If you don't like them, I have others.

Groucho: Hey!

Martha: Now, in the spirit of fairness, let's quiz former Senator and Vice President Joe Biden. Sir, how many letters are there in the word 'jobs?'

Biden: Three.

Audience: HA HA HA HA HA HA HA HA HA HA HA.

Ryan: (muttering) How many syllables in 'moron?'

Chico: Good one.

Martha: That was uncalled for, Burl.

Ryan: Oh, you should hear what I *wanted* to say.

Biden: And this administration is prepared to go the gates of hell to do it.

Everyone on the planet: Huh?

Biden: Oh, wait. I read the wrong canned response.

Harpo: ...

Groucho: I know. This guy's too dumb for words.

Chico: Too dumb? He may be three dumb.

Harpo: (honk)

Chico: Sorry.

Ryan: While we wait for Captain Snicker's meds to kick in, let me just point out that the Medica...

Martha: Time's up, Carl.

Ryan: Paul. *(sigh)*

Martha: Whatever.

Biden: HA HA HA HA HA HA HA HA HA HA HA HA HA HA HA HA HA HA HA HA.

International Blue Velvet

Odd goings-on among many-legged animals
<>~<>~~~~~~~~~~<>~<>~~~~~~~~~~<>~<>

This past weekend, I had the rare opportunity to combine several disparate activities in a single location, a circumstance which doesn't necessarily qualify as an attraction to someone like me - someone who works from home, but thinks even *that* represents a suffocating and cloyingly-structured invasion of privacy.

Bill of Barry's Rights violations aside, however - this past weekend, I had a chance to experience, in one place, things you might not normally expect to find in one place. It was like watching Joe Pesci playing Gandalf in 'Lords of the Flatbush Rings,' or going to a Joe Biden foreign policy presser and stumbling over a cogent thought.

What and where, you ask? This past weekend, I visited a small town in North Carolina, where I spent the day alternating between watching where I was walking, questioning what I just heard, and wondering what I just ate.

Now, before I go on, let me lodge this complimentary disclaimer about the 'other' Carolina. If you're not familiar with the state of North Carolina, know this - it has wonderful edges.

North Carolina's western sector is nothing short of glorious; it's a wildly popular area known to millions of tourists as the scenic Blue Ridge Parkway and Appalachian Trail, and known to a former South Carolina governor as Argentina. And some three to four hours' drive due east, the state's Crystal Coast hosts Cape Fear, Kitty Hawk, the Outer Banks, and the occasional feral hurricane.

In-between those edges, however, you're likely to run into all sorts of scary creatures, species that are focused on nothing but their own survival, like black bears, timber rattlers, and John Edwards.

But don't get me wrong - there's plenty to do in the slow-sloping zone, the tilting plain connecting west to east in North Carolina. For example, North Carolina may have more privately-owned small businesses per square foot than any other state in the Union, if you don't count Congress. North Carolina is rife with unique vendors, peppering the roadsides along winding pavings that lead from here to there, open and ready to serve you on the eight calendar days per annum that the freeways aren't under construction, or under a rockslide.

And specialized, super-niche marketers they are, too! I know of no other state where you can find a business establishment named 'Stumps and Stuff.' (Imagine, just for a whimsical moment, what the 'stuff' might be, in a roadside emporium where 'stumps' got top billing.)

Now, given the fact that we're talking about North Carolina, I should clarify. For the purposes of my story, when I say *'small town,'* I mean *'small'* as in very few traffic lights, and even fewer meth labs. I mean *'small'* as in less than three furniture factory outlets, which, in North Carolina, is small indeed. But for the purposes of my story, I do *not* mean *'small'* in the sense of 'it's hard to conceive of a place this remote that doesn't have actual icebergs.' Although, in North Carolina, such places exist.

In North Carolina, there's a place called Frank, Unincorporated.
That's small.

No, the event I attended took place in a standardly small town, one of those places commonly known as a tourist trap. You know the symptoms:

- Flavored ice vendors with names like The Merchant of Ven-Ice
- A compact town square lined with coy, gingerbread-y gift shops and booksellers specializing in regional titles like *'A Beginner's Guide To Our Indigenous Toads'* and *'The Collective Porn of Carl Sandburg'*
- Frighteningly cute artisan studios with names like 'Barrel Streep' and 'Kiln Me Softly'
- Flavored ice vendors with names like SnoConi
- Dozens of A-frame chalet rental offices, all staffed with realtors named 'Tink' or 'Dovie'
- Slant-in parking spaces, angling in to abut smiley-faced $4-per-hour parking meters

- A perennial-planter-cordoned 'public space,' constantly hosting some bogus festival or another, like the Regional Pit Bull Rapid Response EMT Challenge, or the Orthodontic Late-Bloomers' Clogging Semi-Finals, or The 'Y'all Ain't From Here, Are Ya?' Plaid Bermuda Shorts Fashion Parade & Double-Aught Taillight Target Open
- Flavored ice vendors with names like Sacco & Vanzetti

The event I attended was something known to insiders as an 'equestrian competition,' a term which, for the rest of us, loosely translates into regular English as 'standing in the rain, sipping tepid, Pentagon-project-priced coffee and eating lard-coated tealight candles flash-dipped in fried grease, while young American girls dressed like so many midget British royals coax large mammals around an arid, Grapes-of-Wrath-ish dust-cloud-cloaked arena, in hopes of getting the snorting beasts to negotiate a complex, weaving obstacle course of Lilliputian fences, while onlookers weigh the risks of going for another cup of coffee from the concession stand, some 300 threatening yards away, accessible only after navigating a staggeringly complex, Flicka-dropping-laced mine field, sadistically sown by guerilla recruits from the Clydesdale Contras.'

And as I watched, and dripped, and sipped, and ate lard-wrapped lard, all I could think about was what the horses must be thinking, as they hopped over these faux fences, over and over again. I'm sure the horses were *dying* to point out a few things to the bipeds on their backs.

"Excuse me, up there being all top-of-the-food-chain and stuff - you *do* realize that we could just walk *around* these things, right? It's not a real fence; at least, not a real *long* fence. You *have* noticed they're only about eight feet wide, haven't you, Hoss Cartwright? Hello?"

So, for this summer's family getaway, consider a trip to North Carolina's "Voted Number One" city! It's easy to find - after all, there are something like 114 of it. And don't forget to stop by Stumps and Stuff!

Stumps and Stuff. It's just around the bend from Frank.

Because you can never have too many stuff.

That Darn Joe!

He's wild! He's wacky! He's one heartbeat away from our nuclear codes!
<>~<>~~~~~~~~~~<>~<>~~~~~~~~~~<>~<>

Okay, this week, let's start with a joke:

Joe Biden.
[rim shot]

Yeah, you're right. That's not entirely fair. Let's add a little context:

Joe Biden spoke.
[rim shot]

Get ready for it, citizens: Joe Biden, the unchallenged champ of "he said *WHAT?*" is back for an all-new round of speech spasms. True, "Boo-Boo" Biden's always been hovering in the wings, forever floating about the perimeter, keeping a kettle of klutz simmering on the stove. But now that it's re-election season, Joe and his patented Random Gaffe Generator will be all over the place; that is, unless he goes totally off the reservation and his party's puppet-masters decide to "seal his records."

Some beltway insiders are conjecturing that if Joe Biden doesn't mind his mouth and curtail that urge to ad lib, his next job might be as a Lake Michigan reef.
[rim shot]

Yes, now that the 2012 Olympics have wrapped, Americans are awash in that other grueling, obsessive, every-four-year competition: upgrading our iPhones.

I'm kidding, of course. I'm talking about a *different* circus that's come to town - that three-ring rubber-room insanity known as presidential politics. As if the faked, not-really-live, live Olympic coverage wasn't bad enough (and it was), we now have to put up with parties, platforms, promises, position papers, polls, policies, pandering, pundits and politicians.

Politicians...that unpredictable subclass of upright mammals (well, usually) equipped with a special set of gifts:

- Teeth so bright they require their own sunglasses
- Hair that could double as a South Florida hurricane shelter
- The uncanny ability to simultaneously shake your hand, pat your child's head, wave at donors, and extract your wallet, with only two arms (well, usually), and do it all while smiling, spending money, and promising not to spend money

And now you and I are being force-fed a bottomless broth of political coverage-slash-cheerleading-slash-analysis-slash-opinion, unless, sometime just after the *last* election, you took the clever, preemptive action of cutting off your head. Even then, though, you're probably not safe - some zealous TV pundit would still find you, tap out the most recent poll results on your chest cavity, and ask you for a donation.

(Yes, I know. You cut off your head. You don't *have* ears to *ask*. They don't care.)

Look, here's some professional advice, and I'll be honest (grab the honesty while you can - if our topic is politics, we won't be seeing much of *that*). If you ever decide to write a humor column, politics is the easiest possible topic. Also, politics is the hardest possible topic. (Yes, I know. A lot of my professional advice is like that.)

Writing about politics is hard, because no matter what you write, you've immediately alienated half the country. It's like picking sides in a family argument, or saying you like Batman more than Superman, or eating at Chick-fil-A.

On the other hand, writing about politics is easy, thanks to the huge, endlessly-renewable pool of material.

Which brings us back to our unrestrained friend, Joe Biden, the Incredible Shrinking Asset.

Now, to be fair, Joe's hardly the only politician who regularly chews on his own feet. It's just that he won't shut up long enough for us to go write about anybody else.

For example, when Mitt Romney announced Congressman Paul Ryan as his Vice Presidential pick, Romney goofed and introduced Ryan as "the next President of the United States."

History was made today on the political front, when GOP candidate Mitt Romney, who kills women and is not a real Christian (or even worse, is) announced his running mate: Paul Ryan, a congenial Wisconsinite who likes fishing, camping, and pushing grandmothers off cliffs. For the first time in history, a Party has simultaneously nominated two misogynistic murderers for the White House!
[rim shot]

True, Barack Obama made the exact same mistake some 4 years ago, introducing Joe Biden as "the next President of the United States." The difference is, when Obama announced that Biden was President, the entire state of Virginia committed suicide.

And then, not to be outdone, Joe Biden hopped on stage and referred to his running mate as "Barack America."

It's a gift. Boo-Boo's in a class of his own.

Today, at a presser in Topeka, North Virginia, Joe Biden unveiled his own health care plan for Seniors. But then he dropped it. Aides say it was hours before they got the smell of Chivas out of the carpet.
[rim shot]

In fact, during one recent speech, Biden went so blank that people thought he was a tobacco executive. Joe forgot who his opponent was (he called him "Governor" Ryan). He forgot what state he was in (Virginia). He even forgot what century he was in (this one).

Today, at a campaign rally in Bangor, Kentucky, Joe Biden challenged the foreign policy credentials of his opponent, Monsignor Meg Ryan. Then Joe

wowed the crowd with a rousing rendition of the Prince classic, "We're gonna party like it's 1899."
[rim shot]

And Boo-Boo doesn't just go blank; he goes blankety-blank, too. Joe's shell-shocked handlers lightheartedly refer to his azure vocabulary as having "a firm commitment to adjective equality." You or I would call it "swearing like Joe Pesci channeling Chris Rock at a Quentin Tarantino audition."

The upcoming televised debate between Biden and Ryan may be the first debate in history to require an FCC-mandated five-second delay.

Paul Ryan, by the way, was selected as Romney's running mate some sixteen days before the Republican's national convention. Those that watch such things say it was an unusually early pick, a history-changing statistic if ever there was one, and I wanted to share that with you in case you're not unconscious yet.

The political junkies rushed to point out that it was the earliest a Veep pick has ever been Veep-picked, except for the 2004 election, when John Kerry inexplicably tapped John Edwards, that well-groomed testament to testosterone. (The Edwards pick may have been rushed by necessity, since Kerry had to catch him in-between hair appointments and heir appointments.)

And while we're on the subject of oddly-shaped heads, let's give a nod to Nancy Pelosi, that strangely grinning, seemingly eternal Congressional fixture who now claims that the ghost of Susan B. Anthony speaks to her in the White House. That may or may not be true, but it's still no excuse for a grown woman to walk around Washington with coins sticking out of her ears, especially a woman who walks like some sorority pledge prank victim whose pantsuit legs were sewn together at the knees. Basically, Nancy's a cross between Kathy Bates in "Misery," Lucy Ricardo off her medication, and the Tasmanian Devil on crack.

Nancy's no longer a threat to become an Oval Office occupant, but not that long ago, she was third in line to be President, and the fact that Nostradamus never saw *that* coming is why I don't own any 'Nostradamus Rules' t-shirts.

One final note about Boo-Boo: in 2008, Biden himself got the Veep nod from Obama only *two days* before the convention, possibly because Joe was hunkered down at his home in Memphis, Delaware, reading a comic book about the War of 1712 and watching the CBS news magazine "90 Minutes" with his wife, June Bidet.

Today, during an unplanned visit to Chicago, Vice President Joe Biden announced that he was withdrawing from the election campaign, due to experiencing a severe case of natural causes after running backwards at high speed into several dozen bullets. Biden referred to Taking the Big Dirt Nap as a "temporary setback" - after all, he can still vote and, as everybody knows, nobody messes with Joe.

[rim shot]

Wicca Leaks

Calling the first day of summer 'MidSummer' was a clue.
<>~<>~~~~~~~~~~<>~<>~~~~~~~~~~<>~<>

What does the first day of summer mean to you?

- Anticipation: only 604,822 more seconds till college football season
- Aggravation: the electricity part (A/C) of your utility bill skyrockets...but the gas part (heat) doesn't drop.
- Reruns: remember all those network TV shows that sucked last fall? They're back, they *still* suck, *and* now it's hot outside, too.
- Summer vacations: that annual road trip where the family spends 2-8 weeks driving around America looking at famous Civil War latrines, in-between eating fried lard omelets and four-decade-old pecan logs at 5,000 identical, insipid exit-ramp restaurant/gift shops, as the children forget the Fifth Commandment, and the parents struggle with the Sixth.
- Pagan rituals (*see 'summer vacations'*)

Here in America, the first day of summer is relatively low-key...compared to other places and other times. Throughout the years, summer's first day has been feted by groups as diverse as Druids and Wiccans, Mayans and Aztecs, the Vikings, the Chinese, the Black Panther/Paula Deen Coalition, and Cubs fans.

Traditionally, summer begins on a day called the "solstice," an ancient Latin term combining the words "Sol" (the Sun) and "stice" (more than one sti). Astrologically speaking, the summer solstice is the longest day of the year, except for the day you had that introductory lunch with your fiancée's mother.

Of course, many cultures celebrate the sun, since almost every culture has, at one time or another, looked up. Across the world, the first day of summer is also known as MidSummer, Alban Hefin, Feill-Sheathain, Whit Sunday, and my personal favorite: Thing-tide.

"Bill! How's it going?"
"Same old. You?"
"Well, I've got that gastric thing flaring up again - crazy - had to hose dow..."
"Wow, look at the time! Look, Ted, I gotta get go..."
"You guys doing anything special for Thing-tide?"

As every public school student knows on the day of the test and then promptly forgets, our calendar is peppered with days that cultures have used to mark the procession of seasons: the solstice (summer & winter); the equinox (vernal & dorsal); laundry day; Super Bowl Sunday; Labor Day Weekend; National Civil War Latrine Remembrance Half-Hour.

When Americans hear "summer solstice," normally we immediately think of the Druids, or beer. But by doing so, we cheat ourselves of some fabulous history, much of it deliciously stupid. Witness:

Centuries ago in China, before they discovered American debt, the Chinese had to actually work, and grow their own food. In those ancient days, they welcomed the summer solstice with a ceremony honoring the earth, femininity, and the "yin" part of the yin-yang force. (Yang was celebrated at the winter solstice, with an alternate focus on the heavens, masculinity, and Connecticut real estate.)

In ancient Greece, solstice marked the one-month countdown to something they called "the Olympics," an athletic competition between naked, alabaster-colored men who had zero body fat and no pupils, if you can believe the statues. This 30-day heads-up gave Olympian hopefuls plenty of time to dope up on steroids. (or, as it was known back then, to "get they Spartan on")

The Grecian summer-welcoming festival was called Kronia, during which slaves were treated as equals from 2pm to about 3:15. Kronia was just one of hundreds of festivals on the Hellenic calendar, but I guess that's to be expected in a culture that lets guys run around in the nude tossing spears and stone Frisbees.

Meanwhile, the neighboring Romans were celebrating Vestalia, which paid tribute to Vesta, the goddess of the hearth. Yes, that's what I said: hearth. They had a god in charge of nothing but ashes and andirons. (Those Romans were deity maniacs -

they had specialty gods for *everything*. In ancient Rome, being a god was like working in the US government, but with less corruption.)

The annual Vestalian fun included sacrificing an unborn calf, which you'd have to admit would be a tricky proposition, then or now. (relevant god: Plannus Parenthoodus)

(Initially, Vesta was also the Roman goddess in charge of guarding virginity. But once those Greeks next door invented the college fraternity system, Vesta resigned her chastity commission.)

Elsewhere in Europe, pagan rituals took on regional flavors. In Germany, the land that gave us beer, lederhosen, and men named 'Helmut,' MidSummer was welcomed with raging bonfires. (relevant god: Safetyhelmut Firehosen) Other pagans would celebrate by staying up all night, beering and paganing till dawn, which is were we get the term "frat haus."

The ancient French called solstice the Feast of Epona, in honor of Epona, the patron goddess of horses and mules. During the festival, the French would raise prices, whine about all the boorish American tourists who were ruining things for everybody, and then they would surrender to a mule.

In Lithuania, MidSummer revelers would roll a wheel up a hill, soak it in tar, cover it with straw, set the wheel on fire, and shove the flaming thing back down the hill in the river, as one might do when there's nothing on but reruns. Some of the more enthusiastic villagers would run alongside the wheel as it clambered down the hillside, leaping back and forth over the flames. (*see 'college fraternity'*)

Vikings, they say, used to meet at summer's onset to resolve disputes, attend insensitivity seminars, and try to spell "Minnesota." Massive crowds would gather to vote for their favorites in that year's "Who Wants To Marry A Pillager!"

Also associated with MidSummer is St. John's Day, a day commemorating John the Baptist, who created the casserole and the hot dish supper. On St. John's Day, nervous pagans wore protective garlands of herbs and flowers to ward off evil spirits and other college groups. One favorite plant was called "chase-devil," a plant we now know as St. John's Wort, and which is still used today as a "mood stabilizer" by pungent, liberated women who wear loose clothing, forget to finish their sentences, and have names like Chrysalis and BeBe.

It's true that solstice was also observed in the Americas, but very little is known about summer's importance to, say, the Aztecs, because the minute any enterprising reporter started to scribble, some roving coca leaf-jacked Panther Deity would pop up and pull out the guy's heart.

But despite all this fascinating history - some of it actually true - let's not deny the Druids their due. After all, that's the image we always conjure: Druids at Stonehenge, humming tunes by Pink Floyd.

On the other hand, recent research confirms that, while the Druids *did* lead MidSummer rituals, those rituals did *not* take place at Stonehenge. And...well, let's be honest...Druids without Stonehenge is about as interesting as an Aztec Panther Deity whose wife's making him order the salad bar.

And then there's the Wiccans.

For those of you who don't know, Wicca is a "modern pagan, witchcraft religion" that "promotes oneness with all that exists" and has an agricultural policy that's based on "naked women walking through gardens." Wiccans also worship a "pregnant Godddess," though they can't spell her.

Maybe it's just me, but I'm always a bit cautious about signing on with cults that claim to know the secrets of the universe, but who can't grasp the mysteries of the Great Pregnant Spellcheck Godd.

The Wiccans refer to MidSummer as "Litha" (*literal translation: 'Thing-tide'*). Litha is typically a time for weddings (*see 'pregnant goddess'*) or handfasting (don't ask).

Whatever your Wiccan interests, it's a busy calendar during Litha: there's the crowning of the Sun King, the death of the Oak King, the ascension of the Holly King, Alan King, & Larry King, and the ordeal of "the Green Man" (*literal translation: 'Al Gore'*).

According to one Wiccan website, Litha is truly a madcap time, almost as antic-rich as Samhain (*Buck-Naked Hay Baling*) and Beltane (*Mule Fetus Appreciation Day*), though not quite as out-of-control as Lughnassadh. (*Fraternity Pledge Week*)

For more information on your lucrative career as a white witch, check out the jaw-droppingly ugly and furiously un-spellchecked Wiccan website at twopagans.com. (I guess pagans-r-us.com was already taken.) Be sure to click on the Litha Vamp. And don't forget to visit their Adoptions Page!

By the way, the website domain onepagan.com is still available. But don't dawdle...some franchise-minded Panther Deity is gonna snap that up.

Happy summer!

Stylin' with Genghis

How the US mail got in the US mall

<>~<>~~~~~~~~~~<>~<>~~~~~~~~~~<>~<>

All right, you tell me how you'd handle it.

Picture it. You're the chief suit-in-charge at the United States Post Office, and you're in trouble. You're losing $25 million dollars a day. Every. Single. Day. Your financial track record is abysmal:

- You haven't posted a profit since Benjamin Franklin retired.
- You somehow managed to lose money, even when you were a monopoly. *A monopoly.*
- You're the only enterprise in the history of economics that *raises* its prices (stamps) when demand goes *down*.

Not that you care: you work for the government! You've got so much tenure, you'll still be leisurely pre-sorting L.L. Bean catalogs when the only life forms left on Earth are cockroaches, Twinkies, and Geraldo Rivera (he *refuses* to go away). Plus, you own several pairs of those thick-woven blue-grey government-issue short pants, with the matching knee socks and the Orlando-retirement-community rubber-soled walking shoes. And to top it all off, you're the only people in America who get to drive on the wrong side of the road without getting arrested for being under the influence of Lance Armstrong.

So, in order to at least grasp at solvency, which of the following time-honored business decisions do you choose?

- Reducing overhead costs
- Increasing operating efficiency
- Selling your own line of clothes

I know - that one was way too easy. Obviously, when your mission statement involves moving envelopes from one place to another, and things aren't going well, you get back to basics.

You sell t-shirts.

Yes, the United States Postal Service, the organization that brought you collectible treasures like the "Nudist Appreciation Month" commemorative stamp has decided to design its own line of clothing, because when you're hired by the Post Office, one of the first things they do to you is surgically remove your Irony gene.

According to reports, the hip new clothing collection will be called "Rain Heat & Snow." I guess "Hot Damp & Frigid" was already taken.

Of course, the Rain Heat & Snow line will offer more than just t-shirts. There will be t-shirts *and* baseball caps, in a striking array of colors ranging from "Continental Dusk" (blue-grey) to "Azure Stampede" (blue-grey). This is in keeping with the Post

Office's long tradition of diverse product options (think small boxes *and* big boxes).

Now, don't get me wrong. I'm only tsk-tsk-ing at USPS management here. I'm sure that front-line postal employees are very decent people, including my neighborhood's postal carrier, a very nice lady whose name, I think, is Genghis. Genghis weighs 710 pounds and she smiled once, in 1974. In my neighborhood, if a car is blocking a mailbox on her route, Genghis will actually idle in place, if necessary for several days, waiting for somebody to move the car, rather than Genghis having to actually get out of her vehicle and walk around the offending car. *(Maybe it's a union thing, or a Labor Board violation. Maybe Genghis hasn't yet earned her Orlando shoes.)*

The Post Office was just one of many inventions that were inventioned by Benjamin Franklin. His original idea was to set up a place, preferably an uninspired square brick building with confusing parking and very lame landscaping, where large nondescript men could be inert around a Franklin stove while they recovered from various forms of kite-induced electrocution. This is pretty much what they do at the Post Office today, I suppose; after all, it's just not that easy to lose 25 million bucks a day without active intervention by Congress.

In his portraits, Franklin is always wearing that same, half-pained, half-bored expression, a long-suffering semi-smirk that seemed to say, "Whoa. You're a special kind of idiot, aren't you." It was as if every portrait of Ben Franklin had been painted while he was watching a Joe Biden speech.

But Ben was an amazingly creative and prolific person, what some would call a polymath. (literal translation: "parrot with a calculator")

Most people, unless they went to public school in Detroit, know about Ben's more famous inventions: the Post Office, the Franklin stove, the lightning rod, bifocals (which he invented after mistaking his stove for a Post Office, and leaning against the Post Office). But did you know he also invented the odometer, and the flexible catheter? (They were separate inventions, of course. Not even a practical joking polymath would put an odometer on a catheter. Not with all those Puritans around.)

A note to guys: to avoid any recurring nightmares, do not -- repeat -- DO NOT spend more than five seconds thinking about life during the age of non-flexible catheters. Just let it go.

Scuba fins? Invented by Benjamin Franklin. However, in his first iteration, he strapped them to his hands. Then he invented bifocals, saw he stupid he looked, and put the fins on his feet. The rest is history.

But learning how to not drown, ghost-writing clever quips by Poor Richard, and de-Stephen King-ing catheterization was not enough for ol' Ben. Citizen Franklin made his mark on the music world, too. He invented a glass harmonica, and he charted the first map of the Gulf Stream, which trimmed two weeks off trans-Atlantic travel time, resulting in the Beatles arriving in America two weeks earlier than they otherwise might have done.

In 1775, Franklin was installed as the first Postmaster General, probably as a punishment for dreaming the thing up. Ron Paul immediately showed up and demanded that General Franklin bring his troops home.

Historical Sidebar: We don't know why our Founding Fathers decided to use the term "General" for somebody in charge of the Post Office. For that matter, we don't get "Surgeon General," either, or why, with all these perfectly good generals running about, they then left wars, fighting, and defense to a "Secretary." But the Founders were forever doing weird stuff, like writing an 'f' and claiming it was an 's,' or wearing knickers in public. History is dim on such "why" revelations, but we have a strong suspicion that the Sam Adams brewery was involved.

In 1847, the Post Office issued the first postage stamp. Later that same day, the Post Office issued the first postage stamp price increase.

The Pony Express was established around 1860, but as it turned out, there was very little demand for next-day-delivery ponies. Plus, nobody could figure out where to stick the stamp.

The first airmail flight took off in 1918. Sadly, it would be another ten years before anybody invented airport approach lighting. For all we know, it's still up there, running desperately low on little bags of peanuts.

In 1974, the Post Office began testing an innovative new idea: self-adhesive stamps. And in a classic case of glacial government bureaucracy, the testing of such a complex, radical, quantum-jumpy technology -stamps you didn't have to lick - hummed right along. *For the next eighteen years.*

Seriously. Eighteen years, to test...no-lick glue. Finally, in 1992, self-adhesive stamps were introduced to the self-adhesive-hungry American public. Later that day, Lance Armstrong was arrested for trying to self-sniff the adhesive.

Source: these fascinating facts about the history of the US Postal Service are available at about.usps.com, except for the ones I made up.

And now it's February 2013, and in an effort to save money, the Post Office has decided to open a clothing boutique. Oh yeah - and they've announced they're going to stop delivering mail on Saturdays...

...but not till October.

That's how efficient *this* crowd is: it took them eighteen years to not lick a stamp. And now, it's gonna take 'em six months to *not* deliver the mail.

Ben must be mighty proud.

Six months. Let's just hope that when that ObamaCare disaster kicks in, the Post Office isn't in charge of catheters.

The Frumpy Psychic Network

2013: after 2012, how bad could it be, right? Right?
Hello?
<>~<>~~~~~~~~~~<>~<>~~~~~~~~~~<>~<>

Some time lately, I fell down and hit my head. I'm not sure exactly when it happened, because I hit my head.

Now that, by itself, is hardly news. At my age, I'm clumsier than Inspector Clouseau in a roomful of rakes. On the Graceful-Meter, I rank somewhere between the Three Stooges and the Four Horseman.

But this time, when I came to, I discovered that all that skull jostling had left me changed in two very dramatic ways:

1. I could predict the future
2. I was Secretary of State

Understand - I didn't *want* to be Secretary of State; apparently, this is just something that happens to you if you fall down often enough. But there I was, rubbing my head and wearing a frumpy pantsuit.

But despite my waking up as a woman, with globe-trotting credentials and bad hair, predicting the future turned out to be a bit of a let-down. Kind of dull. Pedestrian. On the other hand, should anybody challenge my predictions, I can just glide into Victim Crusader Mode and start yelling about gender bias and glass ceilings.

Disappointing, this future-gazing. Nothing useful, of course. No tips on sports scores or long-odds horses at the track. No early warnings about globe-altering events, like a meteor strike or the next iPhone. I'm not seeing any hot stock tips or hog market forecasts. No pork belly futures, other than the obvious future for a pork belly...bacon.

No, my prescience is apparently limited to current events...or, technically, what *will* be current events, eventually. Witness:

- The entertainment world will be stunned when Director Tim Burton releases a movie that doesn't star Johnny Depp. Not to be outdone, Francis Ford Coppola will make a picture without DeNiro *or* DiCaprio.
- An NFL player will face a two-year suspension for not having any tattoos.
- Shortly after being subpoenaed by Congress, Hillary Clinton will fall down and bruise her recollection.
- A European study will conclude that those new curlicue light bulbs may cause cancer in kitchen countertops. Congress will respond by outlawing kitchens, and taxing darkness.
- MSNBC will run a story blaming George Bush for denying liberals equal access to dietary fiber. An upstate New York newspaper will post the addresses of all residents who have occasional irregularity.

- President Barry Hussein Barack Soetoro Obama will decline an invitation to show up at his Inauguration Part Deux, opting instead to simply read stuff from his teleprompters, set up on a golf course in a non-Right-To-Work state. Aretha Franklin will again be asked to pretend she's singing, and will again show up wearing a hat that looks like some kind of bad accident between two turtle doves and a galactic star cruiser.

- Two strangers will meet on Craigslist and agree to have a child together. The arrangement will quickly sour, however, when both participants turn out to be the same person, a pre-acne kid from Encino. The kid will end up getting his own reality show, "Two or a Half Men."

- Just before testifying, Hillary Clinton will fall down and suffer a severe diplomatic immunity.

- Because five people in a Seattle commune don't like what the other 312 million Americans celebrate every December, Christmas will finally be outlawed. This will signal the end for thousands of shopping malls, filled with clothing stores that sells ugly sweaters, Christmas tree farms, garden centers that shamelessly peddle those "Seven Disney Dwarves of Christmas" lawn ornaments, and whoever it is that makes tinsel. (nobody really knows)

- Al Gore will sell 14 pounds of his excess head fat to al Jazeera TV's version of the "Lifetime Channel." In their season opener, guest host Richard Simmons will demonstrate how to burn off those pesky lard jowls in his Arab Street hit, "Sweatin' with the Mullahs."

- A college in South Carolina will offer the first-ever four-year degree in Social Media. In keeping with current trends in public education, students will not be graded, as such harsh judgments could damage their fragile egos. Instead, each student's performance will be judged on the number of "likes" they get; at graduation, their GPA's will be assigned a smiley or a frowny face.

- Glenn Beck will offer to buy the internet from Al Gore.

- Joe Biden will not make a single gaffe for 24 consecutive hours, a personal record for America's "special" Uncle. The next day, however, as a result of such unnatural restraint, Joe will unleash a blue torrent so vile that it will cause Quentin Tarantino and Samuel Jackson to break down in tears.

- MSNBC will run a story blaming George Bush after a liberal gets fired simply for refusing to follow the company's dress code, and some embezzlement. An upstate New York newspaper will post the addresses of all residents who occasionally watch TV in their underwear.

- Glenn Beck will offer to buy Al Gore.

- A distracted school librarian will read the entire Obama HealthCare bill by mistake. After the paramedics revive her, she'll report that the first page begins with "Once upon a time" and the last page wraps things up nicely with "And they all died happily ever after." (In-between, there's a bunch of stuff about imaginary doctors, evil accountants, and magic beans.)

- Just prior to testifying, Hillary Clinton will fall down and break everything but her silence.

- The sports world will be stunned when seven-time Tour de France champion Lance Armstrong's second head goes rogue; the cyclist's additional mouth will admit to years of scarfing down performance-enhancing chemicals, including steroids, those little Five-Hour Energy things, and spinach right out of the can.

- Glenn Beck will offer to buy Al Gore's Nobel prize. Al Gore will offer to buy Glenn Beck lunch, and then renege. MSNBC will run a story about Glenn Beck being a racist for using the word "renege."

- Congress will pass a Hurricane Sandy victim relief bill which, oddly enough, fails to include any victim relief. Fortunately for the hard-hit victims, though, the bill *will* include a federal grant for bat guano research at Carlsbad Caverns, and provide much-needed funding for indigent camel care in Qatar.

- Bruce Willis will star in the 47th "Die Hard" sequel, a cross-marketing effort titled "The Walking Dead Don't Die, But If They Did, They Would Die Hard."

- China will call in our debt, and demand we hand over the Louisiana Purchase. But the territory will be protected by the "Duck Dynasty" cast, who will lead an ad hoc militia of sweet tea-fueled bearded men, all calling each other "Jack."

- Congress will pass a law without exempting themselves from it.

- No, they won't. I just made that up.

- MSNBC will run a story about a liberal who fell down the steps, probably after being pushed by George Bush. An upstate New York newspaper will post the addresses of all residents who have a porch.

- Texas, South Carolina, and Lake Michigan will secede from the Union and form their own country, known as "The Semi-Automatic Bible Belt Loop."

- In Greece, a desperate treasury official will list the entire city of Athens for sale on eBay. Amazon.com will outbid everybody else, but the deal will fall apart when Amazon insists on free shipping.

- Barely minutes before testifying, Hillary Clinton will fall down and hurt someone else's head.
- In a very confused show of force, Iran will pave the Gulf of Hormuz. The resulting oil shortage will lead members of Congress to outlaw all air travel, except for members of Congress.
- Plagued with increasing player injuries, the NFL will require that all offensive backs and wide receivers learn how to fall down like Hillary Clinton.

As you can see, it's going to be a long year. Sorry to bring you such glum prophecies, but, hey - don't shoot the messenger. It's not like I made this stuff up.

Besides, this is no bed of roses for me, either. Remember - I've got to add a New Year's resolution to lose some weight, so I won't look so frumpy.

Elephant Talk

An imaginary GOP convention...from an imaginary non-GOP POV

<>~<>~~~~~~~~~~~<>~<>~~~~~~~~~~~<>~<>

Emcee: "Good evening, gentlemen and gentlemen, and welcome to our gala Corporate-Sponsored Middle Class Hate-Fest and Offshore Grandma Abattoir, aka the 2012 Republican National Convention!"

(sounds of 50,000 rich old white men cheering)

Emcee: "My name is Reince Priebus - seriously, that's my name - and I'm Chairman of the RNC, not to mention the only person in America whose name can be rearranged to spell Eerie Crib Puns."

(sounds of 50,000 rich old white men applauding)

Emcee: "And now I, Ripe Siren Cube, am honored to convene the 2012 convention by hammering this ceremonial gavel on a large wooden platform painted to look like the Middle Class."

(sounds of 50,000 rich old white men trying to say 'woot')

Emcee: "Unfortunately, there is a hurricane bearing down on the Gulf Coast, so now I, Brie Snipe Cure, postpone this convention until tomorrow, or Tuesday, whichever comes first. Smoke 'em if you got 'em."

(sounds of 50,000 rich old white men misdialing an Ybor City escort service)

EDITOR'S NOTE: As it turned out, it was a good week to avoid Tampa altogether. After all, the Gulf Coast city was about to be besieged from all sides:
Hurricane Isaac creeping up from the South
Trouble-minded Occupy Movement trailer trash scumming in from the East
That simple idiot Joe Biden being flown in from the North to stage some kind of foul-mouthed Disruptathon, as though, in addition to Isaac, Tampa needed another windbag
And 50,000 Republicans descending from everywhere, which generated a severe condiment shortage among the local restaurants - there's just not enough catsup on Earth for that many expense-account-funded fried-shrimp-eating God-fearing gun-toters.

(Tuesday)
Emcee: "Okay, folks, welcome back. I'm Epic Rube Siren, and if the hurricane season will back off for a minute, I hereby reconvene this convention, where we plan to nominate Governor Mitt Romney, a man cleverly referred to as 'Mittens' by liberals, and third-graders.

(short animated film of Mitt Romney stealing mittens from senior citizens and distributing them to an all-white Olympic dressage team in the Cayman Islands)

Emcee: "During this week, we'll hear from several women, minorities, and various 'people of color,' even though we hate them. We'll hear from Ann Romney, an aloof, out-of-touch 'corporate wife' who lives off her spouse's wealth, has never worked a day in her life, and who only puts on shoes when she needs to kick the help. Oh, wait - that's John Kerry. We'll also be joined by people like Condoleezza Rice, a black woman who, despite being on the faculty at Stanford, having a seat on several boards of directors, being a member of the National Security Council, having been selected as Secretary of State, and having performed with cellist Yo-Yo Ma, refuses to admit that she doesn't stand a chance of succeeding in America without the cradle-to-grave protection of the Democrat Party's Nanny State."

(Low, muttering sound of Joe Biden cursing, though it may have had nothing to do with this humor column. You know Joe.)

Emcee: "But first things first: right now, let's listen to some people talk and make gestures, and then we'll watch some professionally-produced, emotion-invoking video advertisements for our candidate, all of which will attempt to present the candidate as a product - a timesaver, a hot blouse, a shiny new car, whatever - that you simply cannot live without."

(upbeat intro music from a bunch of guys that look suspiciously like David Letterman's house band)

Emcee: "Folks, please welcome Speaker of the House, John Boehner."

(several minutes of what was either Boehner's speech, a low-frequency feedback hum, or one of your more atonal medieval monastery chants)

Emcee: "Thank you, Speaker, for that speech, during which your voice almost modulated. We appreciate you coming all the way from Washington, and for bringing both of your facial expressions."

(sprinklings of applause, interspersed with those unmistakable unscrewing sounds of hotel mini-bar minibottles)

Emcee: "Folks, after hearing that speech, I think we can all agree on one thing: forget voter IDs - what this country needs is a way to identify people who can't tell a joke!"

(sounds of 'Amen!' and 'Here! Here!' and 'Waitress!')

Emcee: "And speaking of laugh riots, please welcome Senator Mitch 'Mitch' McConnell to the stage!"

(several minutes of oration, and the cold truth is this: we're not going to repeat it here. We simply don't have the heart to put you through that.)

Emcee: "Thank you, Senator McConnell. *Man.* What a stem-winder, eh, folks? And I thought *Al Gore* had no rhythm! That may be the whitest five minutes I ever heard in my life. I'm gonna go out a limb here and guess that Big Mitch never moonlighted, scoring rhythm tracks for Morris Day and the

Time. Whoa. My man McConnell makes Mel Torme sound like George Clinton and the P-Funk All-Stars."

(suddenly, the taped sounds of spaghetti western music)

Emcee: "Well, look! It's Clint Eastwood and an empty chair, overtly symbolizing the current occupant of the Oval Office in an existential and pejorative manner that's sure to infuriate Chris Matthews, that hypertensive Barackolyte over at MSNBC!"

(Insane applause, which gets even louder after some under-medicated conventioneer starts chanting 'Sergio Leone for President!')

Clint: "Do you want another four years?"
("NO!")
Clint: "Do you want Boehner to tell another joke?"
("NO!")
Clint: "Do you realize that, during his speech, Jeb Bush mentioned milk eleven times?"
("NO!")
Clint: "If I say 'Make my day,' will you collectively act like nobody has ever uttered three more inspiring words in the history of mankind?"
("NO! I mean, uh, "YES!")
Clint: "Just for kicks, somebody go tell Ellen Barkin I shot the chair."

(sounds of the audience chanting 'No more years!' - which makes no sense until you remember the previous hotel mini-bar reference)

EDITOR'S NOTE: Reviews of Eastwood's 'empty chair' skit were mixed; however, it turns out that the chair had a more cohesive economic policy than the current President.

Emcee: "Well, that wraps up our convention. Thanks for coming, don't forget to vote, and remember this: our candidate has undercoating, comes with A/C and complimentary floor mats, and gets more miles to the gallon than the competition! In closing, please enjoy this unimaginably expensive display of balloons falling from the ceiling. On behalf of rich old white men, I'm Beer's Epic Ruin, saying 'good night' from Tampa."

EDITOR'S NOTE: We apologize for all the Reince Priebus jokes, but if you think *that's* bad, just wait till the *other* convention - we hear the Democrats have somebody named Dick Harpootlian.

Whoa.

Stuck in the Spin Cycle

Look, if I'd have wanted the truth, I'd have made some up.

<>~<>~~~~~~~~~~<>~<>~~~~~~~~~~<>~<>

"230 miles per gallon."

That's what I read on the internet. And just after reading that on the internet, it hit me. In this world, a whole lot of stupid begins with "that's what I read on the internet."

The quote was part of an online discussion about the Chevy Volt, that "hybrid" car that will run on gastricity, as soon as somebody invents some. (Okay, it'll *walk* on gastricity. If you go by these consumer reviews, to claim that the Volt "runs" is to scratch a poetic itch.)

To be fair, though, the Volt is groundbreaking in many ways; for example, this is the first car in history that everybody paid for, but nobody bought.

And, of course, we have the wide-eyed Volt fan I mentioned earlier, who claims he's getting 230 miles to the gallon. From such a statement, we can draw a few conclusions:

- Somebody out there is buying electricity by the gallon
- No, you *can't* fix stupid, but you *can* medicate it into a stupor
- There's a reason we never get visits from intelligent alien life forms

See, one of the great things about the internet is that people can say whatever they want. And one of the worst things about the internet is that people can say whatever they want. Take, for example, another Volt owner who got so disgusted with what he called his "GM econobox POS" that he rushed out to a Ford dealership, bought something large, loud, and dependable that still runs on extinct Jurassic Park extras distilled down into black goo; then he shoved the Volt in his truck's glove-box, drove home, cut the Volt in half with a grapefruit knife, and fed it to his two goldfish, Crockett and Tubbs.

Responsible Journalism Disclaimer: the previous paragraph is only partially true. No respectable goldfish would admit to being named after characters from *Miami Vice*.

But what's even more fun to watch is how the "professional" news media have been handling the developing story of this hard-luck hybrid, with all its Gordian political coilings, its fable-worthy funding, and its pathologically unbalanced balance sheet.

Here's how it works. Let's say the actual news is this:
GM Announces Sale of Second Chevy Volt

Here's what we might see/hear/read...

... from ABC: Hybrid Car Survives Conservative Counter-Offensive

... from NBC: Earth-Saving Technology Embraced by an Enlightened Few

... from Fox News: After the break - more of our interview with Chevy Chase!

... from CNN: White House Confirms Detroit Firmly On the Rebound

... from MSNBC: Volt Sales Double!

So let's take a few actual headlines, and then hand them off to various news outlets for their "analysis."

Responsible Journalism Disclaimer: the nouns in the following paragraphs have not been exhaustively researched, and may or may not represent actual facts. (Probably not.) The verbs, however, are all true.

Okay. Let's begin:

~-~-~-~-~-~

Here's the actual headline:
GM's Volt Sales Up in May

And the media says...

ABC: Volt Continues To Log Record-Breaking Sales Numbers
Fox News: After the break - more people who drove cars during May!
CNN: White House Denies Fleet Purchase of 10,000 Volts

(Glenn) Beck-TV: My next guest will analyze historical trends in auto sales on one of these blackboards.

MSNBC: Obama-Backed Wonder-Car Singlehandedly Revives US Auto Market

~-~-~-~-~-~

Headline:
Surprising June Sales for Volt

ABC: GM Electric Car Exceeding All Expectations, Dealers Say

Fox News: We'll be right back with June Lockhart, and more electronic gift ideas for Father's Day!

CNN: White House Denies Leasing 10,000-Car Fleet from Itself

Beck-TV: My next guest has just written a fascinating book about clandestine electrocution.

MSNBC: Outdated 'Adam Smith' Theories Scrubbed From Textbooks, Replaced With Obamanomics

~-~-~-~-~-~

Headline:
Volt Records Second-Best Sales Month

ABC: Volt Sales Skyrocket Despite Anti-Technology Legacy of George Bush

Fox News: After this commercial break, our list of the second-best movies of all time!

CNN: White House Points Out That Leasing 10,000-Car Fleet to Itself Saved or Created 10,000 IRS Jobs

Beck-TV: We should've seen this coming, as these assorted M&Ms clearly show.

MSNBC: Obama Administration to Fund Chevy Volt Ads in All 57 States

~.~.~.~.~.~.~

Headline:

Chevy Volt Leading US Plug-In Car Sales

ABC: Chevy Volt Catapults to Insurmountable Lead in US Plug-In Car Sales

Fox News: At the bottom of the hour, we'll talk to someone who's pretty sure *there is no other US plug-in car!*

CNN: White House Announces Funding for Really Long Extension Cords

Beck-TV: Don't miss next week's show, when I plan to change tennis shoes and partially shave.

MSNBC: Poll Shows Joe Biden Leading Among US Plug-In Vice Presidents

~.~.~.~.~.~.~

Headline:

Volt's Power Source Compared to Electric Battery Technology from 1897

ABC: According to unconfirmed sources, Republican operatives may have a century-long record of secretly draining Democratic dry cells

Fox News: After the break, Geraldo Rivera will join us, because it's been over an hour since he injected himself into a news story.

CNN: White House Denies Volt Battery Shortcomings; Responds to Controversy by Driving a Giant Gas-Guzzling Black Campaign Bus to Attend a Pro-Hispanic Gay Pride Rally at a Unionized Planned Parenthood facility in an Election Swing State

Beck-TV: Mark my words - it's gonna blow up. I cover this and much more in my new book, *Stuff I Said In My Last Book Was Gonna Blow Up, But Didn't.*

MSNBC: Vatican Admits to Obama Infallibility; Fannie Mae Announces Plans to Foreclose On Catholic Global Real Estate Holdings

~-~-~-~-~-~

Headline:
GM Admits to "Little or No Profit" on Volt Project

ABC: Volt Sales Gracefully Plateau; Unconfirmed Rumor Points to Electricity Boycott by Tea Party

Fox News: In our next segment, we'll take a look at all the successful Government investments since 1897. Should take about eight seconds.

CNN: White House Denies Exploratory Committee's Plan to Outlaw the Term "Recoup"

Beck-TV: Did I mention I have a new book?

MSNBC: Tonight, on an all-new edition of "Slow-Pitch!" Join host organism Chris Matthews and his tingly leg, as we fawn over full-color shots of Barack Obama selecting a five-iron!

~-~-~-~-~-~-~

Let's do one more, shall we?

Responsible Journalism Disclaimer: the following paragraph is true. Well, right up to the part that says "Headline." After that, you're pretty much on your own.

~-~-~-~-~-~-~

Headline:
Exploding Volt Battery Blamed for Over 10,000 Casualties

ABC: Battery Company's Quality Assurance Inspector May Have Tea Party Affiliation
Fox News: After the break, Geraldo describes how he once blew up!
CNN: White House Claims To Have Reduced Highway Clutter By Nearly 11,000 Vehicles
Beck-TV: See? Told you it was gonna blow up.
MSNBC: Obama-Backed Wonder-Car Singlehandedly Revives US Fire Extinguisher Market

~-~-~-~-~-~-~

Welcome to the Umpire State!

Maybe Bloomberg will get confused and ban himself
<>~<>~~~~~~~~~~<>~<>~~~~~~~~~~<>~<>

"Psst."

"Hey, man. What's up?"

"You seen Joey?"

"Joey? Nah, Joey's down in Brooklyn, movin' some fried onion rings."

"Aw, man."

"Why? What you need? I got some nice glazed donuts. Maybe some salted peanuts? 24-ounce Big Gulp?"

"I was hoping to score an unabridged dictionary."

"Yeah, you and me both, dude. Haven't seen one of th..."

"Ack! Cheez it! It's the Mayor!"

~-~-~-~-~-~

I don't know if you've been keeping up with the news out of New York lately, but parts of it have been infected by the dreaded I-Know-What's-Best virus, a particularly foul strain known as the Creeping Bloomberg. This man-nanny is making a career out of irritating people, especially if you're one of those odd, selfish people who think they can choose their own food without ... ready? ... *without the advice and consent of the government.* Or maybe you're one of those irresponsible jerks who insist on running around unattended, just buying whatever size soft drink suits your fancy. Imagine!

This Bloomberg guy somehow got it in his duly elected head that his divine purpose as Mayor of the Big Apple is to incessantly nag and niggle about stuff - as if New York City were just some great big grade school, with tunnels and very tall classrooms, and he's the smarmy little snitch that Teacher made hall monitor.

And ever since, he keeps pointing at things and barking "No!" He keeps at his crusade to make things go away: cigarettes; guns; salt; sweets and sodas; funny Saturday Night Live skits.

But, apparently, micro-managing public consumption isn't enough for the Nannies of New York. They weren't satisfied with controlling the stuff you put in your mouth; now, they're going after the stuff coming out of your mouth, too.

Now, the New York City Department of Education wants to ban words.

Not all words, of course. Society still needs some words, words like *please, thank you,* and *Duck!* And I'm sure the phrase "Vote for me" will warrant a waiver from the Word Police, as will "Please donate to my campaign" and "No, Your Honor, I don't recall."

They'll make allowances for the business world, too. Construction workers would look silly using nothing but sign language to make rude remarks whenever a woman walks by.

And cabbies can't just hold up curse-slathered signs every time they need to, um, advise some pedestrian. That might distract them from, um, interpreting red lights.

And they're not banning words everywhere. (Yet.) First, they're focusing on 'tweaking' the language that educators use when designing tests for school students. According to a school chancellor, the goal is just to make sure test makers are 'sensitive' when developing test questions.

So, educators are busily reviewing your child's standardized tests, in an effort to excise anything that might possibly confuse, upset, or offend anybody. Anywhere. Ever.

And I mean *anybody*.

For example: according to the new uber-nanny Sensitivity guidelines, tests shouldn't include any references that suggest 'wealth,' because that might stir up feelings of jealousy that could permanently scar the little darlings. (I'm guessing if the little darlings knew you were honestly afraid to use the word 'wealth' on a test, that might stir up feelings of "you are an idiot.")

Testers should also avoid references to expensive gifts, vacations, and prizes, because, well, not everybody has won a prize in their life, now, have they? (which is pretty much the whole *point* of a prize, isn't it, idiot?)

And whatever you do, don't mention that...now, hang on to something...some houses on Earth have...a swimming pool.

You break that news, and those poor dysfunctional kids'll be pulling out the rice mats and ceremonial suicide swords.

According to the guidelines, you *can* mention computers...to a point. Computers are okay, but only in the context of school or work. I suppose it would just be too overwhelming for a child to discover that some people own a computer - especially if the kid discovered it while texting from her Droid Razr about a Flickr image upload to her facebook account, or learned it from a re-tweeted Google search on her Bluetoothed iPad.

Birthdays are now a taboo subject, because birthdays aren't celebrated by Jehovah's Witnesses. (I'm gonna go out on a limb here and speculate that there's never been a twelve-week TV miniseries entitled, "More Fun Things Celebrated By Jehovah's Witnesses.")

In a related story: you can't say 'dinosaur' any more, because dinosaurs suggest evolution, which might offend creationists. But you can't discuss the idea of an intelligent, created universe, because that might offend evolutionists. (I'm speaking figuratively, of course. Dinosaurs didn't actually *suggest* evolution. Very few dinosaurs could carry on an intelligent conversation; somebody would get started, but then somebody would start eating somebody else, so nothing productive ever got done. It was a lot like today's Congress, except the dinosaurs finally went away.)

Based on Bloomberg's 'banned words' list, New York City itself couldn't exist. The word 'city' smacks of a smug, anti-rural bias, the word 'new' could upset juveniles whose parents can't afford new stuff, and 'York' might offend sergeants, or people who harbor deep-seated anxiety issues about peppermint patties.

Dancing is now a trauma-inducing topic, but ballet isn't. So I suppose if you came up with a test question that involved John Travolta at a disco in a leisure suit and a tutu, you might slip that one past the censors.

Or how about Jennifer Grey and Patrick Swayze, burning up the '63 Catskills in 'Dirty Pas de Deux.'

Now you're talking trauma.

Animal shelters are out: they're now considered overly traumatic. But let's be honest: if you were forced to make a choice between going to an animal shelter or going to a ballet, what line would *you* be in?

Here's a partial list of New York's new childhood-psyche-searing topics:

- Alcohol and drugs (They meant to exempt some cocktails, but nobody knew how to spell 'Margarita')
- Birthdays (here's an idea - the next time a Jehovah's Witness rings your doorbell on a Saturday morning, answer the door in ballet tights, carrying a Margarita and a birthday cake)
- Bodily functions (Seriously? Surely this topic was *already* off-limits?)
- Celebrities (especially celebrities who have bodily functions)

- Death (although death is a crackerjack way to cut back on birthdays)
- Gambling that involves money (I guess gambling's okay if it involves sheep, or small fruit)
- Halloween (How come you never see any Jehovah's Witness costumes?)
- Natural disasters (Look, if you brag about *your* hurricane, then everybody'll want one.)
- Religious festivals (We're still waiting for a ruling on the obscure but wildly popular 'Feast of Saint Pterodactyl')
- Rock-and-Roll music (They actually added the word 'music.' These people are pitiful.)

But look: we need to be prepared. If this All-Up-In-Your-Business virus continues to spread; if the Nanny Polizei ultimately get their way; if we're really going to start banning words, then somebody needs to get busy coming up with a bunch of replacement words.

Otherwise, our _____ is _____, and we're all _____.

Unsound Bites

Well, it's nearly here. In fact, for many of you, by the time you get around to reading this, it will all be over. All across America, men, women, and single guys will have done that thing that Americans do every four years:

Vacuum.

No, I'm talking of course about America's Presidential election - that joyous period when we all pull together in some kind of collective national psychosis, a sort of interstate insanity, as we try to convince ourselves that anybody who would spend a billion dollars to land a job that pays $400K is honest, competent, and/or sane (any single quality will do, and sometimes even getting *that* can be tricky).

In America, we vote. Voting is one of our inalienable rights, like unlimited calling plans, or $9 birth control. Voting is what we call a political 'franchise,' because politics is a lot like a fast food drive-thru, except politics smells worse (and the drive-thru's out of order). Plus, in political franchises, the restaurant asks *you* for seconds.

And every four years or so, we elect a new President, whose job it is to get re-elected while avoiding felonious behavior in intern-rich environments. But most importantly, the President's task is to maintain his golf handicap and equally represent everyone. ('Everyone' is a complex political term, broadly defined as 'people who donated to my campaign.')

We're very proud of this 'President' idea. See, here in America, we would never put with the concept of royalty: some family who claims divine authority, sets up a ruling structure, and then pretty much ignores us. No, here in America, we elect representatives: exceptional, upright adults who literally swear to look out for our best interests.

And *then* they ignore us.

Americans, therefore, take voting very seriously; so seriously, in fact, that some people aren't satisfied with voting just the one time. And so, in the media, you'll often see voting anecdotes involving men, women, young people, dead people, cats, a brace of oxen (both named Swizzle), and undocumented workers from Somalia who don't speak English but somehow still arranged for a group bus to carry them to polling places in central Ohio so they could vote early, collect $20 from a Union guy named Tony, and take the bus home.

Case in point: according to one internet reporter, in this year's Presidential election quarterback Tom Brady has voted early some twenty-eight times. (We know it was quarterback Tom Brady, because on all twenty-eight bogus voter registration cards, he listed his legal name as "Quarterback Tom Brady" -

even in the three precincts where he showed up as a woman. Wow ... what a Patriot!)

Voting in America has not only created career politicians; voting has created voting careers, that exist solely to gin up more voting. It's like that picture of a snake feeding itself by eating itself, or a great big set of teeth trying to grow more teeth by eating other teeth. But let's not drag Joe Biden into this.

Here, for example, are a few of the cottage industries spawned by the franchise we call voting:

Robo-Calls

I'm sure you already know all about this foul, evil technology, especially if you live in what politicians refer to as a 'swing State.' A robo-call is a robot that selects your phone number from a database and then uses another robot to dial your phone, at a time determined by a junior assistant robot as the most inconvenient possible moment of your evening, which then triggers yet another robot to play a script of a human voice urging you to vote for Candidate X (who, as far as you can tell, is also a robot).

Over the years, several politicians have mounted election campaigns based on promises to outlaw robo-calling. But the simple-headed pols always used robo-calling to gauge voters' anger at using robo-calling, which eventually caused everybody involved to explode in a massive irony fireball.

Yard Signs

There are only two occasions in American society when people ever put signs in their yards: political elections and yard sales. (There used to be a third occasion: For Sale signs. But due to bonehead decisions made by politicians elected in political elections, nobody anymore can sell their house.)

A candidate's yard signs seem to have very little actual effect on political races; in fact, the primary value of yard signs is the role they play in generating a need for replacement yard signs. (see the article 'Vandalism and Cheap Beer: A Study in Feedback Loops' at PlannedParenthood.gov)

Voter Mobilization Groups

These are (usually) local offices, (usually) bound to the mission of getting more people to vote. At their best, they assist potential voters in the registration process, and help legally registered voters access the correct polling places. At their worst, they become vote zombies who will gnaw their way through radioactive concrete in order to get Candidate X elected. But let's not drag Hillary Clinton into this.

One example is the controversial group known as ACORN, a dimly-lit collective, blissfully free from the ravages of ethics, and monitored by federal authorities about as frequently as continental drift. ACORN is like an urban version of the Khmer Rouge, but with indoor plumbing.

~-~-~-~-~-~

Sadly, voting has become so important that it's also attracted society's underbelly (but let's not drag personal injury lawyers who glue 4-inch-square refrigerator magnets all over the front cover of your phone book into this). Our political history is scarred with episodes of voter fraud, especially as various States have become more and more lenient about who can take part in 'early voting.'

For instance, in Massachusetts and parts of Vermont, you can now register to vote as a fetus, as long as you have a clean police record and make a small donation to Planned Parenthood. (a process known as 'late-term extortion')

Earlier this week, we learned that Attorney General Eric Withholder and his Department of Just Us were heading to Florida to keep an eye out for voter fraud (see 'irony overload').

Oh yeah, that'll work. That's like sending Paula Deen to guard a spiral-cut ham.

But remember, voting is your civic responsibility, especially if you're an undocumented illegal alien house pet, or you're dead.

Why, even our own President took a quick moment, after bogeying the fifteenth hole, to urge old people to vote early, in case they died before getting to exercise their Obama-given right to vote for him on Election Day.

And even if you do die, no worries. Go to Chicago, where you can be dead and still vote. If you need a ride to Chi-Town, borrow the Somali's bus.

Just don't get cremated. Remember, it's gonna be four more years before I vacuum.

The Second Second Coming

Even from deep space, this year's Democratic convention was weird

<>~<>~~~~~~~~~~<>~<>~~~~~~~~~~~<>~<>

"Artxsnkl?"

No reply. The long dark starship was silent. Jmkorgpld raised his voices.

"ARTXSNKL?"
"Yo!"
"I just pinged another one."
"Can you classify it?"
"Not yet. But I got an aura sample."
"Sweet. Galactigoogle it, and let me know. I'll be in the regenerator."

Jmkorgpld swiped his desk clean, strapped into his work spine, and jacked in to the computer console. The wavy little logo blinked on, and then the console announced, "Hello, Jmkorgpld. Thank you for using Windows 7.65^{79} x $10.5E8$ (Service Pack 2). Please wait." A surge, and the wall lights dimmed and pulsed. As usual.

"Unbelievable," carped Jmkorgpld to himself. "We can bend time and space, but we still can't figure out how to run a torsotop *and* the regenerator at the same time. If we had any peer species, I'd be embarrassed."

Jmkorgpld attached two leads, knuckled the 'Analyze' glyph, and watched his data manifest. After an irritating light-dimming second, the screen spoke.

"Based on my analysis of your input aura, you appear to have picked up a modulated signal from a seriously remote source: the planet Terra, which is, like, 3 bus transfers from here. The aura's abnormally high emotion signature matches my previously stored patterns of something Terrans call a 'DNC convention'."

Jmkorgpld clapped two of his hands. A Terran political convention! What a find! They'd waited four light years since the last one!

Democrat politics. All the religious fervor of a Southern tent revival, but without the deity. A current-day Caligula festival, plus funny hats.

" Artxsnkl, I got a hit. It's Terra again."
"Terra. Why does that name sound familiar? Isn't that the planet that still uses politics?"
"They were. Now they've switched to something called 'international martial law.'"
"Well, they never were very bright, were they. Got a clean, steady signal?"
"You thinking what I'm thinking?"

"Madcap Mantra Movie night!"

"All the classic comedians! John Kerry! Jesse Jackson! "

"Maxine Waters! Joe Biden!"

"Groucho Marx!"

"You wish. Okay, cue it up, Jmkorgpld."

(And now, thanks to the miracle of time compaction, combined with warp travel and a total disregard for facts, we bring you a bit of what Jmkorgpld and Artxsnkl saw...)

~-~-~-~-~-~-~~-~-~-~-~-~

The sole purpose of the 2012 DNC convention was to re-anoint their Main Man, the main event, Barack Barry Hussein Soetoro Obama, for a second term as President. And prior to the convention's kickoff, the convention center's exterior had been ornamented by a 16-foot-tall sand sculpture of the main event, Barack Barry Hussein Soetoro Obama.

The man erected a statue to himself.

Unfortunately, rainstorms damaged part of the DNC's little Mount Rushmorelet. At first glance, it appeared the rain had washed away Obama's right side. But then somebody pointed out that Obama doesn't *have* a right side.

~-~-~-~-~-~

Despite threatening to overwhelm the convention with 10,000 confused smelly people holding misspelled signs, the Occupy movement slouched into town with about 800 people wearing a total of $7 in retro clothing. Unfortunately, nobody had remembered to bring any food, so naturally the Occupiers started demanding free food from the city. The ·city refused, but they did give the Occupiers a few pairs of John Kerry's flip-flops.

~-~-~-~-~-~

Facing huge drops in attendance, convention planners reneged on their rental of an entire football stadium, gave away buckets of event tickets, and ultimately had to bus in college students and entire black church congregations, and a container of raw meat for the Occupiers. A reporter noticed an empty "Department of Corrections" bus idling outside the convention hall, but given the week's list of guest speakers, the bus could've been dropping off or picking up.

~-~-~-~-~-~

Nancy Pelosi was not the first to speak on-stage; she was, however, the only speaker to refer to Barack Barry Hussein Soetoro Obama as "that brilliant hunk of man-flesh." She went on to applaud some obscure, unread Health Care law that provides free contraception to coeds by taxing the sale of your home.

According to her, Barack Barry Hussein Soetoro Obama is Earth's only hope to stop those one-eyed slavering Republicans and their godless attempts to curb women's reproductive rights. (Republicans deny this charge, saying a woman can reproduct all over the place if they so choose - just bring your checkbook.)

~-~-~-~-~-~

Speaking of 'godless,' the Democrats got badly scalded after somebody removed the words 'God' and 'Jerusalem' from the party's official platform. So, in a bold bipartisan gesture, the delegates consulted some polls and then voted to amend their platform by inserting the words 'Santa' and 'Wolfie's Deli.'

(There was an unsubstantiated rumor that Republicans had floated a fake poll, showing that a vital voting bloc, single hermaphroditic neo-Hispanic mothers with lactose issues and a mortgage-backed Pell Grant, were in favor of Nancy Pelosi wearing spandex leggings and a Hannibal Lector mask. Within minutes, another floor vote was called, and Pelosi was observed trying to pick out a matching pair of shoes.)

~-~-~-~-~-~-~

Everyone looked forward to the "Obama's not the pig I said he was four years ago" speech by Bill Clinton, though, like Pelosi's "bill," nobody knew what was in it. But there was even more buzz *after* the speech, when the crowd learned that Bill had ordered a pizza.

~-~-~-~-~-~-~

The aforementioned coed Sandra Fluke, that contraceptive Gatling gun, apparently found a sex-free moment to speak to the crowd. After the crowd learned more about her, several people *volunteered* to pay for her birth control.

~-~-~-~-~-~-~

The parade of professional policy experts continued, including those crack global economists and time-proven business experts, Scarlett Johansson and Eva Longoria, both of whom set personal records for remaining dressed in public.

~-~-~-~-~-~

At one point, John "Chin Plow" Kerry showed up and - honestly - accused somebody of flip-flopping. Even the *Democrats* snickered at that one. Kerry spoke for a few minutes and then surrendered to the band.

~-~-~-~-~-~

Near the end of the week, there must have been a security glitch at the DNC convention, because Nancy Pelosi managed to get back on stage during a smarmy 'American Dream' video, pretty much confirming the media's mounting concern that this whole week was rapidly spinning out of control. After a few minutes of blinking like a caffeine-crazed ferret, the former Speaker actually said, "Wasn't that American Dream story the story of America?"

Pelosi then caromed back to health care. She began boasting that the new law, which weighs more than most hospitals, would keep women from being a pre-existing condition, whatever that meant. At that point, she was tackled, dragged off-stage, and fed to the Occupiers.

~-~-~-~-~-~

Finally, on Thursday night, the crowd was treated to a short psychotic episode by Joe Biden, aka 'The Incredible Shrinking Asset.' Joe's job was to serve as the warm-up act for his boss and, if possible, not leak any nuclear launch codes. Not surprisingly, therefore, Biden leaked most of Obama's upcoming speech, resulting in about half of America switching to another channel. After all, once Joe had jumped the shark, nobody needed to actually *watch* the speech, so people were free to go take care of more important chores, like folding laundry, or dusting your velvet paintings of Debbie Wasserman Schultz playing poker.

~-~-~-~-~-~

About ninety minutes into his ten-minute speech, Biden's allure was spent, not to mention his opportunities to say "literally" when he meant "virtually." Michelle Obama had this look on her face like she'd swallowed too much wasabi. Finally, during a particularly emotional clause, Biden poked himself in the chest one too many times, and a disgruntled segment of his hair follicles walked off the stage in protest.

~-~-~-~-~-~

Backstage, the week's star speaker, the main event, had been impatiently pacing the wings. Across the room, Obama's ego watched the follicles storm off. It whispered to its host, and Obama spun around. Mistaking the rug remnant for all of his Vice President, the main event made his move.

President Obama took the stage. The straggling die-hards in the remaining crowd tore their garments, MSNBC's Chris

Matthews saw visions, and 241 overweight women in big hats went into spontaneous psychological labor.

Barack Barry Hussein Soetoro Obama began to speak. And after a few minutes, Jmkorgpld paused the spaceship's feed.

~-~-~-~-~-~-~~-~-~-~-~-~

"Artxsnkl , this is practically the same speech he made four years ago!"
"Well, why not? It worked then."
"Point taken. Humans. Oy."
"Any dip left?"

~-~-~-~-~-~-~

Also Sprach Bacon Bits

A tale of pork, protests, and paranormal pari-mutuels
<>~<>~~~~~~~~~<>~<>~~~~~~~~~~<>~<>

Every now and again, some event will occur, a happening of such jaw-dropping significance that history is forever altered, plus there's a spike in business for the struggling Jaw Repair market.

And if you're the alert and lucky soul - if you're paying attention when the window of opportunity knocks on the Cape Cod split-level of metaphor - you get to see it.

Last week, I was that soul.

It was beautiful. A headline for the ages. And if you were a humor columnist, or a diehard fan of the Psychic Friends Network, it was an absolute gift:

Topless Protest Spices Up Psychic Pig's Feeding Time

Yes, I already had a column half-written. Didn't matter. There are times when plans must be put aside. Tactics must be revised, adjustments must be made. Pigs must be consulted.

Here's what we know, at its purest, most distilled level: somewhere in the Ukraine, there's a pig named Funtik, and Funtik is a bookie.

I'm kidding, of course. As a rule, no self-respecting bookie (with or without cloven hooves) would accept wagers in Soviet currency. I mean, the pig's not an idiot.

But these were odd days - all this was happening during the Euro 2012 soccer tournament, and Europe operates by a different set of rules (or symptoms) during soccer season. Picture, if you will, one those cheesy B-film horror movies, where all the residents spend the first half-hour modeling farm-labor fashions, strolling along the main street, and calling each other by their first names, and then suddenly they all contract some brain disease from the local water supply, causing them to set the town on fire, eat each other (by their first names), and re-elect Orrin Hatch.

It's like some continent-spanning, multi-national group psychosis, compounded by people speaking 230 different languages, France surrendering to 229 of 'em, and Greek politicians running around kiting checks.

So when a psychic farm animal started picking futbol winners, Europeans barely blinked.

BACK-STORY SIDEBAR: This extra-sensory-pig story comes to you courtesy of that international news giant, Reuters, which is not pronounced "rooters" for a reason. Reuters is not pronounced "rooters" because my humor column is about a pig, and the universe has a rigidly-imposed irony limit.

Say what you will about our universe - it knows when enough is enough.

According to Reuters, Funtik the pig was selected as the Ukraine's unofficial Euro 2012 mascot because several largely unsupervised Ukrainian soccer fanatics believed Funtik could predict the winning teams in the Euro Cup finals.

BACK-STORY SIDEBAR: It was just this sort of moronic, out-of-control, free-style thinking that led to Vladimir Putin's easy re-election as champion of the Semi-Naked KGB Agent Atop A Party-Sympathetic Horse Party.

Now, as far as we know from the Reuters' story, Funtik had no particularly impressive curriculum vitae, nor did he present a list of stellar references during his interview, although he was once spotted having a light nosh in Laguna Beach with Miss Cleo. And during employee orientation, he did drop Dionne Warwick's name several times.

BACK-STORY SIDEBAR: It should also be noted that Funtik's record as a porcine prognosticator was not all that impressive, which would shock nobody, except maybe Miss Cleo, or maybe those investment geniuses at JPMorgan. ("Look! Our investors lost 2 billion dollars! No, wait! 4 billion! No, wait!")

Twice a day, Funtik's feeders would interrupt the slumbering fellow's musings to bring him two bowls of whatever it is that supernaturally-endowed pigs eat. Each bowl bore the national flag of one of the two futbol teams playing each other that day.

The crowd would wait for Funtik to tuck in, and the flag on the first bowl chosen identified that day's winning country.

And don't you *dare* start judging the Ukrainians. Remember, every February, American humans are perfectly willing to make six weeks of travel plans based on the meteorological expertise of a groundhog.

I'm still not sure how we got to the top of the food chain.

Still and yet, none of this could have occurred unless some local sports fans, gathered at some big-screen-infected post-Soviet saloon, had decided to go with a psychic pig instead of ESPN. Imagine *that* meeting:

Citizen A: I propose that, instead of reading sports column, we should buy pig.
Citizen B: That is brilliant plan.
Citizen A: All in favor, don't say 'nyet.'
Citizen C: But we are Ukraine! We have Chernobyl! Why we can't get our own mutant pig?
Citizen B: That is brilliant plan.
Citizen D: Why are we all talking like Boris from *The Rocky & Bullwinkle Show*?

But on this particular day, says the Reuters report, things got weird, even by European standards. On this day, the Czech Republic squad was scheduled to face off against Team Portugal.

Now, in America, this would be a yawn-fest of channel-changing proportions; a wench-bring-me-caffeine-and-be-quick-about-it moment, the equivalent of a quark-sized college post-season game; say, the Bickering Bisons of Lower Tuna Chancre, Montana, pitted against the Congenital Gophers from Marginal Aptitude, Iowa, in a real nail-biter at the Supplementary Bowel Incision Bowl. (sponsored by the League of Frumpy Plus-Sized Women Voters)

But in Europe, the Portugal-Czech showdown was serious business.

Serious, yes. Not quite as serious, however, as the issues that were irritating a Ukrainian women's rights group known as Femen. (literal translation: League of Frumpy Plus-Sized Women Voters)

And on this day, before Ukraine's finest paranormal wagering pig could get a good aura going, he was interrupted by a Femen-backed dissenter wielding an encrypted brace of breasts. An impromptu push-up protest, if you will. A bare-your-grievances breast-in. A full frontal united front.

Suddenly, as Funtik was getting his slop on and his vibe on, the Femen protester busted up into the pigpen and started getting her strip on (assuming, of course, that they speak hip-hop in the Ukraine).

As reported by Reuters, Femen had been scheming to organize this little pigpen protest with one of their own, a 31-year-old Femen-nazi named Olexandra Nemchinova, who barged in, ripped off her blouse, and bared her "protest placards."

BACK-STORY SIDEBAR: See, Femen felt that the Euro soccer tournament helped promote the sex industry. So, naturally, their response was to interrupt a pig's dinner and lob a half-naked woman into the argument.

Now, as we mentioned, Mizriz Nemchinova's demands were encoded. Sort of. The activist's sweater assets were protesting in a Cyrillic language. Fortunately, we were able to obtain a translation, provided by a roving reporter from Reuters Foreign Desk in Belarus (*"The Bureau Best Abreast of Brest's Best Breasts!"*). According to the translator, the lady's sternum-scrawled screed basically expressed a desire that the Euro 2012 tournament should go perform a highly improbable biologic function upon itself.

In case she hadn't made her point, young Olexandra than began shouting similar (though equally unlikely) suggestions, all designed to crystallize Femen's displeasure with the tournament and its sordid effect on the citizenry. For example, Femen claims the tournament's "fan zone" is nothing more than "a cattle pen for deceived fans who are seduced by swill in the form of beer and mindless entertainment."

As if that was a bad thing. They should see America during football season or, for that matter, at either political party's National Convention.

Shortly, though, the whole thing ended as such things often do: police arrived and carted off the 31-year-old and her two equally 31-year-old, uh, pamphlets.

But for Funtik, life - and lunch - went on. No stranger to the media kliegs, Funtik took the whole thing in stride, assuming, of course, that psychic Ukrainian hip-hop pigs that have seen half-naked slogan-tattooed coed protesters during a Putin administration are allowed to stride.

Funtik sniffed the protestette's discarded blouse, handicapped next year's Kentucky Derby, and spotted Dallas 6 points in the NFL playoffs.

And then he ate Portugal.

Bottom Ten

If a tree falls and hits a Bigfoot, can anyone still hear a lawyer?

<>~<>~~~~~~~~~~<>~<>~~~~~~~~~~~<>~<>

Every now and then, I meet someone who's willing to admit, out loud, that they read my humor columns. If you're one of those six relatives, then you already know that I'm a huge fan of doing research for my columns. (One day, I may actually *apply* some of that research to a column, though probably not.)

I work hard to put together these weekly, occasionally-proofread volleys at literacy. Contrary to what you may think, these columns don't just leap fully formed from my forehead like some spoiled child-god of Zeus, or just suddenly appear like a new zero in Obama's spending spree.

No, I have to do my homework. It's my duty, and it beats vacuuming. I owe it to you, faithful reader, to get my facts straight before I dive into each week's universe-altering topic; soul-stirring subjects like the intertwining history that connects the Twinkie to malt Scotch, or the tale of the former USSR pig that predicts World Cup soccer winners. (I mean "former" as in "pig in an ex-Soviet Republic," not "former" as in "ex-pig." After all, writing about a soccer bookie made out of bacon would just be stupid.)

Besides, intensive research is a luxury I can afford, for two primary reasons:

1. I'm a single guy, and
2. I have Google

Being a single guy is an acquired taste, like malt Scotch, or Rosie O'Donnell. It's not something that simply *happens*, just because you're not married, or not dating, or no longer answering your Caller ID-enabled phone. A guy *is* a bachelor; a guy *learns* to be single.

Being single means learning to cope on one's own, or at least learning not to yell at thin air in public. Believe me, nothing queers a grocery store conversation like suddenly spinning around, pointing your finger at absolutely nothing, and shrieking, *"STOP HUMMING THAT!"*

No, the simple state of matelessness doesn't do it: that's not a single guy; that's a bachelor. A bachelor is "in-between," a single guy is "beyond." *What* he's beyond ... help, hope, corrective medication, clothes that match ... that's a topic for another day.

The point I was trying to make, if I recall, is that single guys, because they're single, have the time for good, solid, in-depth humor column research, and for the record, this may be the first time in the history of literature that anybody has used the words "humor column" and "research" in the same sentence. (It is, without question, the first time anyone has ever referred to *my* stuff as "in-depth.")

And thanks to technology, we now have Google, a company that makes the smallest, smartest research assistants ever born that aren't members of a workers' union. And thanks to some *more* technology (if you have three or four hundred bucks to spare), we can now access Google from our smart phone, which is way better than trying to fit a 26-volume encyclopedia in your jeans pocket.

But when working with Google, you have to watch yourself, because a simple search can take you places you absolutely never intended to go.

Here's an example.

One week, I was "researching" a story about all these advertised drugs that have up to two medical benefits, but a minimum of 414 dangerous side-effects, including nausea, persistent or recurring death, or becoming Rosie O'Donnell.

As part of my (ahem) research, I googled something like "top ten prescription drugs." And after a ridiculous, insufferable wait (0.004 nanoseconds), Google returned some 47,000,000 results for "top ten" stuff.

Google's like that. Serious "over-achiever" issues.

One Top Ten list in particular caught my eye: the Top Ten Strange Topics That Need More Explanation. I clicked through to have a look because, what with being single and everything, I had a noticeable absence of spouses nagging me about some garage-cleaning project that I'd been promising to take care of for six straight months, which I would handle right now if I really cared enough about her, and why don't I ever take her anywhere nice.

The first thing I noticed on the Top Ten Strange Topics That Need More Explanation page was the phrase "State Farm Bethesda." Personally, I couldn't challenge that accusation, having never been in a situation so dire that it would require me to need Maryland-specific insurance.

But the actual "Strange Topics" in the Top Ten list were, I thought, pretty lame. UFOs. Bigfoot. Déjà vu. Mysterious disappearances. Ghosts. Something known as "The Taos Hum," which turned out to be a gender-free organic potter wheezing on her turquoise-encrusted dream-catcher - an octogenarian hippie known to locals as Dakota the Emasculatrix.

Mysterious disappearances? That's rather vague, not to mention redundant. If it wasn't mysterious, it wasn't a disappearance, was it, Mr. or Mrs. Amazing Randy? It just means somebody left - maybe to go clean the garage.

Here's an actual "Mysterious disappearances" quote from the website: "People disappear for various reasons."

Whoa. What well-funded pan-national think tank secured *that* little knowledge nugget?

And Bigfoot? Seriously? Somebody's still calling in Bigfoot sightings? To this day, as far as I know, not one reputable scientist has collected one hair, one tooth, one bone. No Yetilike lair uncovered, no Sasquatch-shaped crop circles, no great big hairy size-nineteen-tennis-shoe road kills.

Not one Bigfoot has ever applied for government benefits. There have been no Bigfoot anti-defamation legal challenges, and no snarky lawsuits filed by the P-ACLU (Proto-American Civil Liberties Union).

Not a single Bigfoot has ever appeared in an episode of Judge Judy, alleging that his dirty stinkin' low-down Bigfoot-in-law knew all along that that Chevy transmission was no good.

And we've seen no rural newspaper Bigfoot obits, noting the untimely passing of prominent Bigfeet:

Oog Bigfoot (age unknown) died at his home (address unknown). Services will be held tomorrow at Mastodon Mortuary, once bright sky light-ball rise above high stone hill where is home of Bear God. The family are receiving non-carnivorous guests at the Bigfoot communal water source (address unknown), refreshments to be provided by Oog's former coworkers from Bigfoot Local #11.

Oog Bigfoot is survived by his most recent she-Foot, Gaa, who works part-time as a claims clerk at State Farm Bethesda, and the two little-Foots, Oog Jr. and Rosie O'Donnell.

The Littlest War

North Korea's latest threat: Death by Photoshop

<>~<>~~~~~~~~~<>~<>~~~~~~~~~<>~<>

December 2025. A third-grade classroom, somewhere in flyover America. The first-period teacher waits a few more moments, mentally calculating the lag time before her students' sedative-laced half-pints of milk kick in. Finally, she rhythmically taps her NEA-issue smart-board-pointer-slash-emergency-Taser against the rim of her 'Genders R 4 Haters' mug.

"Okay, class: settle down. I know you're all excited about getting a few days off for the Wholly Secular Voluntary Deity-Nonspecific Winter Solstice Seasonal Timespan, but first we're going to wrap up our discussion of the Great Korean War of 2013. So let's all turn to page f...Yes, Lauren?"

Lauren: "Mr. or Mrs. Ibn-Juarez, Joey just pointed to a cloud shaped sort of like a gun!"

Joey, a seasoned veteran, instinctively addressed the court. "Did not!"

Mr. or Mrs. Ibn-Juarez stared wistfully at the Taser. "Lauren, please go to the infirmary and have the IRS agent give you a Xanax."

Lauren nodded. "Yes, sir or ma'am."

"And ask the nurse to let you bring back a dose of Ritalin for Joey."

"Hey, this is a gyp!" whined Joey. "My Mom said we can talk about guns all we want, now that Dianne Feinstein's fessed up to that weird affair with Charlton Heston's ghost, when she had his out-of-body child out of wedlock, on the house, off the record."

"It's not just the gun allusion that got you in trouble, Joey. It's the cloud. Remember, references to the weather are now illegal, too."

"Since when?" Joey challenged.

"Since the National Weather Service stole all that ammunition from the Social Security Administration and started firing on white, dreadlock-wearing Rasta-wannabes who insist on surfing during a hurricane."

Joey looped a nonchalant doodle.

"You know, I also saw a cloud that looked like a frustrated androgynous witch stuck in a dead-end teaching job. I'm just sayin'."

"Again with the clouds?" Mr. or Mrs. Ibn-Juarez raised his or her eyebrows. "Strike two, young man."

"You are *so* not gettin' a Winter Solstice card from me this year."

Silently cursing those useless can't-even-get-a-doomsday-right Mayans, Mr. or Mrs. Ibn-Juarez intoned, "Joey Biden III, you are hereby charged with a violation of the Federal Childhood Angst Avoidance Act of 2014. At this point, we would administer your government-mandated punishment, but we can't, because that would be a violation of the Federal Childhood Angst Avoidance Act of 2014."

"Oh, that's rich," Joey commented. "I'd say it's ironic, but you guys don't teach irony till fourth grade."

The teacher bit her lip. "Becky, would you like to read from today's lesson?"

Joey: "Why does Becky always get to read?"

"Because, unlike some future repeat offenders I might mention, Becky doesn't snicker every time somebody says the word 'tentacle.'"

Joey: <snicker>

"That," the teacher muttered, "and the fact that her father's on the School Board's teacher pension review committee."

"Mm-hmm." Joey stared out the window. "Tell me - in fourth grade, will we cover cynicism, too?"

Mr. or Mrs. Ibn-Juarez: "Becky?"

Becky flipped to her bookmark. "Chapter Six: A Gnat on the Pacific Rim"

"Early in the Spring of 2013, North Korea's current Kim (Lil Kim) was sitting at home in the dark, when one of his generals, Lo Phat, told him that 'Pyongyang' is actually a Mandarin slur meaning 'pudgy shrimp.' Incensed, Lil Kim declared war on South Korea, South Dakota, the South Bronx, and Austin, Texas."

"Why Austin?" asked Joey.

Mr. or Mrs. Ibn-Juarez fielded that one. "Apparently, Dennis Rodman jokingly told Lil Kim that Austin is the capital of the USA. At least, we *assume* it was jokingly."

Becky piped in. "And it says here that Lil Kim's battle plan was code-named *Tentacle*."

<snicker>

The teacher tried her best to mask a smile. "Becky, that was unnecessary."

"Sorry," Becky exhaled in a forced stage whisper. *"But Joey Biden's such an idiot!"*

"You should meet his Dad. Please continue."

Becky found her place and continued, reading the following:

For years, military analysts had warned that Lil Kim was closer to nuclear capability than anyone thought. But nobody took Lil Kim seriously, because...well, *look* at him! The guy's got a haircut that makes Shemp from the Three Stooges look like Fabio, he's got more jowls than Jed Clampett's Fourth of July barbecue, and the man would have to stand on a box just to be short. And on top of all that - which in Lil Kim's case is not hard to get to - he's named Kim! It'd be like everybody running around fearing some dictator named Tad.

Plus, everybody figured that if Lil Kim ever got too stupid, China would just conscript about 600 million people's employees from one or another people's Dell Computer sweatshop, march them all across the border into North Korea, and just have them fan out in a great big peninsula-sized people's blob, until there was nowhere left to stand. (Actually, nobody seriously believed this China scenario except the French, who immediately surrendered to Taiwan, and US Secretary of State John "I'll Have To Ask My Wife" Kerry, who immediately surrendered to Dell.)

Then, in March, the world community's fears were confirmed when the North Korean army allegedly launched a missile across the tenuous border into South Korea. To be fair, though, North Korea didn't actually *'launch'* anything, technically speaking; what happened was this: Lil Kim's generals found one of those houseboat pontoons and stenciled the words "IS NUKE BOM" on the side. Then they rounded up 60 plus-sized women laborers who shouldered the pontoon, got a running start, and lobbed the thing over a rust-flecked fence along the 38th Parallel, where it landed in a retaining pond, maiming two non-partisan mallards sent in to observe under UN protection.

Afterwards, Lil Kim's bureau of propaganda (the 'Yoo Duc Now') released several aerial shots of missiles allegedly raining down across South Korea, and Austin. Unfortunately for Lil Kim, North Korea's psychotic little Chia Pet, the pictures released to the world press were immediately discarded as photoshopped shams: in one photo, for instance, riding the several dozen Earth-bound warheads were several dozen wildly whooping Slim Pickenses.

Experts quickly reached a consensus: these were the most obviously photoshopped pix in the history of history manipulation, with the possible exception of that snapshot of Moses accepting a couple stone tablets from Barack Obama.

<the hall door squeaks open>

Lauren: "I'm back!"

"Yes, we see," the teacher admitted. "Now sit down, Lauren, if you can scare up a chair that doesn't remind you of an Uzi. And stop waving your arms."

Lauren squinted edgily. "Why is...why is the wall moving?"

"It's just the Xanax, Lauren. You're hallucinating. Look, run back down to the infirmary and apply for a job as a tax auditor, or Governor of California."

<thudding sound as Lauren almost doesn't run into the wall>

"Better, Lauren. Better all the time, dear."

Mr. or Mrs. Ibn-Juarez took a moment, inspecting her classroom's ceiling, as if there might be some celestial guidance up there in the pencil-pocked drop panels.

"Okay, finish up, Becky."

Becky continued. "Fortunately, a cheesy black-and-white monster from a poorly-dubbed Japanese horror movie showed up and destroyed Lil Kim's secret headquarters with a 1400-degree-Fahrenheit case of projectile halitosis like you cannot *imagine*. And a tentacle."

Joey: <snicker>

Mr. or Mrs. Ibn-Juarez: *"Becky..."*

"Sorry."

Bigfoot's Beret

My, what big genomes you have!

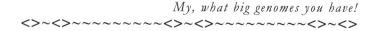

I was driving through a busy neighborhood, eating a burger, changing clothes, and typing a few notes for an upcoming column. And then somebody sent me this sentence:

"When we first looked at the report of the bigfoot genome..."

I dropped the dashboard TV's remote *and* my meth pipe. I nearly stopped texting.

Pardon me? *Whose* genome? Somebody's claiming to have *lab samples?* From *Sasquatch?*

Of course, I had to know more. I pulled into a well-kept daylily bed, picked up some schmuck's unsecured wireless signal, and hopped online. A few googlish taps, and there it was.

A Texas veterinarian was claiming to have gotten her hands on some Sasquatch samples; some bio-forensic artifacts, possibly lifted from a honky-tonk bar's cocktail napkin during "Beast Karaoke Night." (*Ladies and Yetis, No Cover!*)

Not that she's some unqualified, backwater pet Doc who wildly claims to map genomes of a weekend, mind you. She herself admits that she once mapped a horse. (She's not supposed to talk about it, though, since a judgment is still pending.)

The horse had no comment.

As I read on, it quickly became clear that the somber, tenured, career-level, full-time genome posse were challenging Dr. Lone Star's science, all of which was based on a questionable hair sample. The scoffer articles were full of words like "purported," which is how polite evolutionary biogenetic paleoanthropologists say "Oh, you *so* made that crap up." (And, to be fair, entire careers have been spawned from questionable hair. I give you Geraldo Rivera.)

Of course, it didn't help when the genome-moonlighting vet claimed she got her sample ... and I am not good enough to make this stuff up ... she got her sample from "leftover blueberry bagels eaten by a family of ten Bigfoots who live in Michigan."

So now Bigfoot is Jewish. Just like Geraldo.

The scientific community's major concerns about the "purported" Sasquatch Swatch fell into two categories: contamination and scale. In other words, the other scientists alleged that the vet's research team didn't really know what the sample was, and that *whatever* it was, they didn't test much of it - chromosomally speaking. Broadcasting "Bigfoot exists!" based on such rickety evidence would be the height of dishonesty: like a realtor hiding a "This Property Condemned" sign, or Congress passing a law without reading it. Okay, bad example.

Granted, it was easy enough for Team Texas to prove it wasn't a purely *human* hair, thanks to thorough, intensive instruction in forensic research (they almost never missed an episode of *CSI*). But analysis of the bigfoot bouffant was turning up traces of other, unexpected varmints (possum, panda bear, Eliot Spitzer). Obviously, therefore, the sample seemed to be contaminated, unless Eliot Spitzer had ever propositioned a panda - which is not out of the question.

The "scale" accusation was even simpler. Here's the background: Inside the nucleus of each human cell are things called base-pairs, things so small that it would take nearly five of them to make a full-sized French entrée. Base-pairs combine to make proteins, which is a good thing, since French chefs don't do protein. Next, the proteins manufacture designer genes, in very tiny Indonesian slave labor factories, which are then purchased in bulk and resold to "host organisms" (me, you) by "couriers" (Levi Strauss, Liz Claiborne).

The leftover genes combine to make DNA, which is important because this is the first science acronym we've used in this whole article, and I hope you appreciate how hard it is to write a scientific article without lobbing acronyms all over the place. DNA is composed of something called the Double Felix, which is a pair of cartoon ladders that swirl madly together in a tiny, torrid dance until they create chromosomes, or get propositioned by Eliot Spitzer.

And this is where the Texan Puppy Doctrix let science down. See, the *very smallest* human chromosome contains over 40 million mappable base-pairs.

The vet mapped, like, six.

But her defense was that she filled all the gaps by using genetic sequencers. (In Texas, apparently, it's common for vets to keep a nice genetic sequencer or two in the office, just there next to the chew toys.) She claims the sequencers were able to deduce all the missing sections - *all* of 'em - which would be like somebody studying a sandal and, from that, constructing Barack Obama's Middle East foreign policy. Okay, bad example.

Besides that, we've all seen *Jurassic Park*. We know the dangers of genetic sequencing; we know what you can end up with when you start toying with nature. Yes: Jeff Goldblum.

Whatever the purported hair sample belonged to, here are some of the Texas Gene-Riders' purported findings: The sample's *nuclear* genome was a muddled mix of human *and* non-human sequences (rodents, maybe, or game show hosts). But the *mitochondrial* genome - which comes only from the mother - was human. (*Mitochondrial* is a scientific term meaning "if Mama ain't replicatin', ain't *nobody* replicatin'.")

So, Bigfoot's ancestral mother was a human.

Well, well, well. Looks like *Mama* was a rolling stone.

But remember, we're talking about biological species that can (theoretically) interbreed, not just college guys on a lust safari, or Eliot Spitzer. We're talking about mating, not sex. *Any* semi-conscious biped can screw up *sex*. I mean, a guy in Ohio recently got arrested for trying to have sex with a rubber pool raft. In an alley. (Wonder what *that* guy's genome looks like...)

But the vet wasn't through yet. Oh, no. Next, she claimed that Bigfoot's parents had met in France.

As you know, your average scientist subscribes to the theory that Sasquatch originally tromped across an Asian-Alaskan land bridge, managed to not get shot and eaten by the ancestors of Sarah Palin, and finally settled in exurban Seattle, which would explain grunge music. But the vet seems convinced that Mr. Size EEEE took a different route - that he left France, walked across the then-frozen Atlantic, down through Canada, finally settling somewhere in New Jersey, which would explain Chris Christie.

So, in other words, Bigfoot is the result of some hirsute proto-human doing the Humpty Dance with a 13,000-year-old French chick.

Imagine that romantic night along the moon-washed banks of the Seine:

Her: "le Dude. You're, like, everything I ever wanted in an eventual man: you have opposable thumbs, and you walk upright. Well, mostly upright. Okay, needs work. But you *do* have the thumb thing."

Semi-Him: "oog atra muk. spitzer."

Her: "Here's my number. When your appendix goes vestigial, call me."

Chariots of Ire

How yogurt and naked badminton killed the ancient Olympics

<>~<>~~~~~~~~~~<>~<>~~~~~~~~~~<>~<>

Did you watch the Olympics? You did? *How?* Every time I tuned in, somebody was trying to sell me underwear.

Or a President.

As you probably know already, the NBC television network bought the rights to cover the Thirtieth Olympiad which, according to NBC's overworked fact-checking department, is being held in London, the capital of Ontario, California. And according to our fact-checking department (the internet), NBC has officially raked in over $1 billion in advertising sales for this year's Olympics.

NBC has taken an interesting approach to covering the games live from London, which is five hours ahead of New York, 8 hours ahead of LA, and 3,000 years ahead of Detroit, the capital of Iran. All during the day, NBC brought us live coverage of commercials; then in the evenings, during prime time, NBC ran reruns of commercials, peppered with batches of live commercials.

And in-between the daytime and nighttime Olympic coverage, NBC's endlessly-grinning adjective wranglers provided Olympic updates, after warning us that they were providing Olympic updates. These news professionals would actually look into the camera and tell people, "Okay, if you don't wanna know who won, turn your head! Don't look, okay? Ready? Are you sure?"

I've never seen anything like it, except from much shorter people who were wearing shorts and eating a candy necklace.

Leading the pack this year in Olympic commercial buys were some commercial buyers you might not have expected. Sure, there were the ubiquitous spots for sports equipment, power drinks, and personal injury lawyers. But vying for the Gold Medal in "most Olympic advertising dollars" were some strange bedfellows:

1) Chobani yogurt
2) Fruit of the Loom
3) Barack Obama

"Huh? What?" you may be saying, and with a rich vocabulary like that, you're well on your way to a career with MSNBC. But it's true - the current occupant of the White House was in a spending war ... with an underwear factory. Of course, it's not an entirely level playing field: Fruit of the Loom has to buy ad time *with its own money*. And Obama has a kind of home-field advantage, too - according to MSNBC, he actually descended from Mount Olympus.

Michelle "The First Michelle" Obama just happened to be vacationing in London, too, though I suppose that might've been pure coincidence. Maybe she just flew across the Atlantic Ocean to show her support for Fruit of the Loom, or to try and outlaw some English food. But while in London, The First Michelle was interviewed by one of NBC's resident enamel flashers, and in keeping with NBC's coverage of this White House, it was utterly unbiased, probing, and intense.

NBC: Did your brilliant husband say anything inspiring yet today?
TFM: Yes.
NBC: How brilliant is your gorgeous husband?
TFM: Several.
NBC: May I kiss this photo of your miraculous husband?
TFM: Make it snappy.

But even when the peahen network *did* manage to slip a little Olympic coverage into their Olympic coverage, it came off more like some kind of internal competition for Cutest Commentator:

~-~-~-~-~-~

Bod: Good evening, everybody. My name is Bod Costco, and on behalf of NBC, may I welcome you to the 2012 Olympic Games, here in beautiful Athens, the capital of Ontario. We'll be right back.

[Commercial segment that runs longer than CERN's atomic clock]

Bod: Welcome back! I'm Bod Costco. Over the next several weeks, I'll be staring at you with my highly rated, non-threatening wide-eyed expression. Isn't that right, Tweety?

Tweety: That's right, Bod! Hi, everybody! I'm the perky and non-threatening Tweety Shallot, and here we are again at the Beijing Olympics! Yes, the Olympics, that magical time when the world comes together so Americans can make fun of other athletes' names! But since we paid obscene amounts of money to be here in the Scottish capital, let's get right to our commercials!

[Commercial segment that lasts longer than Israel's captivity in Babylon (the capital of Norway)]

Tweety: Welcome back, everybody! Tweety Shallot here, one of several dozen vapid, grinning Journalism majors hired by NBC, based entirely on our outstanding dental work! Over to you, Chaz Charles!

Chaz: Thanks, Tweety Shallot! I'd like to welcome everybody to London, the capital of Wales. I'm Chaz Charles, here with your Olympic weather! But first, these words from our sponsors.

[Commercial segment that takes longer than a phone call for computer software support, if the support center was being run by the DMV, who outsourced it to a US Post Office facility in New Delhi, Ontario]

Bod: That's our show. Good night, America!

[Cue extremely lame electronic keyboard arrangement of the theme from *Chariots of Fire*]

~-~-~-~-~-~

In any case, here are a few Olympic moments, as I recall them, except for the ones I just made up, as if I were NBC's fact-finding department. But bear with me. Given the time zone issues, the language issues, and all the interruptions while I ran to the store in my yogurt to buy more underwear, my Olympian observations may be a bit confused.

~-~-~-~-~-~

- In the very first medal competition of Olympiad XXX, the nation of China (aka Bank of America) won ... hang on to something ... the coveted women's air rifle competition. I know, I know. I'm crushed, too. Now, you be strong, okay? There's always the 2016 Games. Call a friend for support if you have to. Don't let this destroy you.
- Unfortunately for NBC, however, after that breathless thriller, 90% of NBC's worldwide viewing audience switched channels and went back to watching "Dancing with the Real Housewives of the Jersey Shore Network Stars at the Osmond Family Feud Reunion Special, starring Justin Bieber as Betty White."
- Ann Romney's horse, Rafalca, was slated for dressage competition in the Olympic Games, but sources say the animal was a bit out of sorts after having to ride all the way to England on top of the plane.
- Tragedy struck Team USA when swim team member Carrie Nano, a teenager from Topanga Canyon,

electrocuted herself while texting during the 400 meter freestyle.

- Of course, it almost goes without saying that Michael Phelps won another handful of medals. It won't surprise me at all if, one day, we see a headline like this: *Dateline 2060 AD - pseudo-human avatars at the Virtual Olympics went wild as 75-year-old swimming legend Michael Phelps claimed his 54th Medal, after coming in first and third in the Physical Therapy Knee Extension Pool 3-meter dash.*

- In case you missed it, there was a badminton scandal, and that's the first time in all of human history that those two words have ever been used in the same sentence.

- I watched lots of women's beach volleyball (of course, I only watch it for all the well-written articles). I was never sure which team was from where but, based on the uniforms, I'm thinking it was usually Sherwin Williams versus Abercrombie & Fitch.

- On the other hand, watching men's water polo proved to be a bit distracting, since all the guys in the pool were wearing some kind of Nathaniel Hawthorne-ish wimples on their heads. They all looked like half-naked mutant Puritan chambermaids.

- In tennis, women's singles, the legendary Serena Williams and her bionic serve slaughtered a Russian opponent to win the Gold. After the match, three battered, semi-conscious tennis balls filed charges of cruel and unusual punishment.

- A swimming medalist from China denied all charges of "doping," despite being observed at the mouth of the Thames eating krill. After the race, she protested the allegations by sitting at the bottom of the pool for three days.

- A sprinter from the diminutive Marshall Islands raced in front of an Olympic crowd larger than the entire population of his home country! Coincidentally, aging pop star Madonna, following her doctor's advice to cut back, announced that she's dating the Marshall Islands.

- Team USA won a water polo qualifier against Montenegro. I didn't know Montenegro was a country; I thought it was a sandwich.

- For the first time ever, the tiny island republic of Palau was represented at the Olympics. Upon learning that a citizen had left the island nation, Georgia Congressman Hank Johnson started yelling something about the island getting all unbalanced and ultimately tipping over. Johnson was immediately whisked away for observation, and was then re-elected.

- Mitt and Ann Romney went home empty-handed (Ann's horse placed thirteenth), but political pundits say the horse is likely to pick up all of Ohio's electoral votes.

- Of course, there were moments of pure athletic brilliance. I watched a young female Brazilian gymnast perform the most amazing combinations of flips I've ever seen. Had I attempted jumps and landings like that, there'd be nothing left of me but a big pile of "tate" issues - prostate and testate.

- Michael Phelps make some interesting international news, too, when he got a job offer to be the entire Montenegro navy.

- And as if the bad Badminton Mafia story wasn't bad enough, there was more shameful news as three teams from former Soviet republics were caught taking a dive - cameras caught them trying to throw a game, in the fiercely competitive Rock/Paper/Scissors semi-finals, by illegally changing their vote to 'paper.'

~-~-~-~-~-~

So there's our peek into the XXX Games. We'll see you four years from now, at the games in Rio de Ontario (the capital of Manila). Until then, good night, thanks for watching, and don't forget to buy lots of Greek yogurt in your underwear!

ABOUT THE AUTHOR

Barry Parham is a recovering software freelancer and the author of humor columns, essays and short stories. He is a music fanatic and a 1981 honors graduate of the University of Georgia.

Writing awards and recognitions earned by Parham include taking First Place in the November 2009 Writer's Circle Competition, First Prize in the March 2012 writing contest at HumorPress.com, and a plug by the official website of the Erma Bombeck Writers' Workshop. Most recently, Parham's work has appeared in three national humor anthologies.

Author's website
http://www.barryparham.com

@ facebook
http://www.facebook.com/pmWriter

@ Google+
http://tinyurl.com/n6w5gq4

@ Twitter
http://twitter.com/barryparham